Doing Business in the United States

Doing Business in the United States

A Guide for Small Business Entrepreneurs with a Global Mindset

Anatoly Zhuplev
Matthew Stefl
Andrew Rohm

BEP BUSINESS EXPERT PRESS

Doing Business in the United States: A Guide for Small Business Entrepreneurs with a Global Mindset
Copyright © Business Expert Press, LLC, 2018.

First published in 2018 by
Business Expert Press, LLC
222 East 46th Street, New York, NY 10017
www.businessexpertpress.com

ISBN-13: 978-1-94709-820-6 (paperback)
ISBN-13: 978-1-94709-821-3 (e-book)

Business Expert Press International Business Collection

Collection ISSN: 1948-2752 (print)
Collection ISSN: 1948-2760 (electronic)

Cover and interior design by S4Carlisle Publishing Services
Private Ltd., Chennai, India

First edition: 2018

10 9 8 7 6 5 4 3 2 1

Printed in the United States of America.

Abstract

As nations and regions worldwide enter a period of political–economic transformation and undergo changes in accessibility and market potential, the U.S. market remains an attractive destination for entrepreneurs, small and medium size enterprises (SMEs), and other business entities with a global entrepreneurial mind-set. Books and other sources dedicated to starting and doing business in the United States often focus on academic or large corporate audiences, making them less attractive for aspiring entrepreneurs or SMEs with a global attitude setting their sights on the country.

This book strives to serve as a concise guide to understanding the American business landscape from an international business perspective. By and large this book is designated for foreign-based entrepreneurs and SMEs aspiring to expand into the potentially attractive and robust, yet also highly competitive, American market. U.S.-based readers will also find it instrumental and highly relevant in developing their knowledge base and analytical toolbox for perfecting their competitive edge.

The book begins by discussing the process of internationalization of the SME as a competitive strategy. It looks at the pros and cons of expanding internationally from the SME's standpoint and rationalizes international expansion as part of the strategic triad of benefits, costs, and risks. Factual illustrations include cross-country comparisons contrasting the United States with comparator countries in terms of their business attractiveness. The book offers numerous analytical tools and frameworks designated as practical applications addressing key aspects of starting and running a business in the United States. The remaining part of this chapter suggests a practical application grounded in the SME internationalization. This application integrates the main aspects and key components of a background research involved in an SME internationalization decision.

Why the United States? The book shifts to discussing the bright and dark sides of doing business in the United States, including its role and place in the global marketplace and comparative business potential and attractiveness. The costs and risks of starting and doing business in the United States are discussed at the national and regional levels with multiple examples and factual illustrations from California, the largest state characterized by high business potential and a complex socioeconomic–political landscape. Small business and entrepreneurship, its environment, dynamics, and business start-up logistics are examined at the national and regional levels.

Marketing is the heart of any successful business enterprise in the United States and therefore the material in the remainder of the book discusses the fundamentals and contemporary trends and applications in marketing. Chapter 3 examines the challenges in persuading consumers to change attitudes and shift behavior and offers strategies and tactics to help the SME break into the U.S. market and stand out and succeed. In this chapter the book strives to facilitate understanding of the diverse and complex American consumer landscape through the lenses of generational cohorts, geography, and ethnicity. This analysis includes marketing applications and analytical tools such as the 4Cs, SWOT analysis, and additional research resources to better understand market entry opportunities and dynamics within the United States.

Branding, the core of strategic marketing in the United States, is the subject of discussion in the concluding chapter of the book. Building and activating the brand, developing and building a strong and differentiated brand as foundation of any successful market entry strategy, and the marketing mix (product, promotion, place, and price) form the building blocks of the company brand and are designed to convey the customer value proposition and deliver actual customer value. As part of the analytical and factual support featured in the book, the authors discuss the process of measuring, testing, learning, and optimization—called *marketing analytics*—as vital to helping businesses optimize and maximize their marketing mix strategy and execution.

Keywords

branding, business, entrepreneurship, internationalization, market entry, market research, marketing, small business, SME, start-up, strategy, U.S., United States

Contents

Acknowledgments

We would like to acknowledge the help of all the people involved in this project and, particularly, express appreciation to the colleagues at Loyola Marymount University and Business Expert Press for outstanding editorial support.

Anatoly Zhuplev
Matthew Stefl
Andrew Rohm
Loyola Marymount University, U.S.A.

Introduction

The Land of Opportunity

There's gold in them thar hills . . . and there's millions in it.
—Mark Twain (1835–1910), an American writer, humorist,
entrepreneur, publisher, and lecturer.

I just don't like sitting around and waiting and thinking. I always
repeat this: "When you start walking the way, the way appears."
—Hamdi Ulukaya (1972–present), a Turkish businessman,
entrepreneur, investor, and philanthropist of Kurdish
background based in the United States is the owner,
founder, chairman, and CEO of Chobani, the #1-selling
Greek-style yogurt brand in the United States.

Mark Twain's 1892 novel *The American Claimant* portraits a character, Mulberry Sellers, as he appeals to a group of gold miners hungry for fortune—an early staple of American business—to go forth, stake their claim, and strike it rich. As the Chobani quote and success story suggests, over one hundred years later, the United States remains a land of opportunity. That's precisely what Tesco PLC thought in 2007 when, after 20 years of consideration, the British company finally introduced Fresh & Easy supermarkets to the United States. The launch had all the hallmarks for a bright future. Tesco would undoubtedly benefit from its years of experience and success in the United Kingdom, a seasoned team running the expansion, a significant amount of industry research and data, and enormous financial backing (to the tune of $1.5 billion) in addition to a stagnant yet hypercompetitive grocery store landscape in the United States dominated by longtime players, many of whom were perceived as lacking innovation.

Tesco planned to shake up the grocery category by exporting and applying much of what had led to the company's domestic success—fresh items at affordable prices, smaller package sizes, faster self-checkout lanes, a robust selection of ready-made meals, and more. Six years later, however, the company packed up and went home, bloodied and beaten by the tough U.S. grocery battleground. Considering its vast array of resources and assets, how could Tesco have failed?

The economic recession that rocked America in 2008 certainly played a role, but looking back it was evident that there were cracks in Tesco's armor. A number of issues previously identified by Tesco corporate research were overlooked during its U.S. entry, including the challenge of opening aspirational stores in lower-income areas, a very British-tasting ready-made menu, a U.S. market that loves larger, bulk packaging and discounts, and consumers that weren't yet ready for self-checkout. In short, Tesco senior management held numerous assumptions about the U.S. market, its various subcultures, and the American grocery shopping consumer that proved misleading if not false.

Despite its current divided political and legislative climate, the U.S. economy continues to be strong, leading to a market that remains fertile for entry. The world's fourth largest geographic area, in 2016 the United States had the third largest population of 326.6 million people, comprising 4.4 percent of the total world population. The U.S. economy generated $18.6 trillion (or 15.6 percent of the world's total) in gross domestic product (GDP) in 2016 and is ranked 11th worldwide in GDP by purchasing power parity (PPP), the measure of what a common *basket* of consumer goods containing items such as milk or orange juice would cost in various countries. Exports of U.S. goods and services reached $1.471 trillion, or 12 percent of the world total, in 2016 (World Factbook, 2017). By late 2017, low unemployment (at 4.2 percent, Bureau of Labor Statistics, 2017) and high consumer confidence ranging between 95 and 100 percent (Trading Economics, 2017), combined with a thriving business environment, a seemingly insatiable thirst for consumption, and vast spending power, continued to make the U.S. market an attractive entry point for foreign businesses.

With such a fertile and sizeable market, market entry should be a piece of cake, right? Wrong. As we saw with an eminently prepared company like Tesco, the U.S. consumer is diverse, fickle, and complex; the highly regulated U.S. market is flooded with goods, services, brands, and advertising messages; and the competition for the U.S. consumer's attention and share of wallet is fierce. For every market entry success story, there are a thousand failures. It shouldn't be surprising that a survey by U.K.-based Barclay's Bank revealed that 46 percent of retailers surveyed consider the United States to be the most challenging market to enter, compared with China (32 percent), Japan (16 percent), and France (14 percent). With respect to the volume of products that the United States imports ($2.7 trillion in 2016) from foreign countries, the largest categories include B2C[1] products such as apparel and foot-wear as well as technology goods such as mobile phones and televi-sions ($584 billion in imports). Additional import categories include services (e.g., travel and transportation, computer services, banking and insurance), representing just over $500 billion in imports; automo-tive vehicles, parts, and engines ($350 billion); and food and beverages ($130 billion). In 2016, the United States ran a trade deficit of approxi-mately $500 billion as it imported overall more goods and services than it exported.

---

[1] The most common categories of business format include business-to-business (B2B), business-to-consumer (B2C), business-to-government (B2G), business-to-manager (B2M), consumer-to-business (C2B), and consumer-to-consumer (C2C). B2B: Business-to-business describes commerce transactions between businesses, such as between a manufacturer and a wholesaler, or between a wholesaler and a retailer. B2C: Business-to-consumer (sometimes also called Business-to-Customer) describes activi-ties of businesses serving end consumers with products and/or services. B2G: Busi-ness-to-government is a derivative of B2B marketing and often referred to as a market definition of *public sector marketing*, which encompasses marketing products and services to various government levels—including federal, state, and local—through integrated marketing communications techniques such as strategic public relations, branding, marcom, advertising, and web-based communications. B2M: Business-to-manager is a relatively new mode of e-commerce. It refers to transactions between enterprises (product sellers or any other workers) and professional managers. C2B: Consumer-to-business is an electronic commerce business model in which consumers (individuals) offer products and services to companies and the companies pay them (e.g., private households selling solar panel–generated electricity to the grid/utility company). This business model is a reversal of the B2C model. C2C: Consumer-to-consumer (or citizen-to-citizen) commerce involves the electronically facilitated transactions between consumers through some third party (e.g., eBay, Craigslist).

Is succeeding in American business tough? Yes. Is it impossible? No way!

This book is organized in two parts. In Part One (Chapters 1 and 2), you'll learn about internationalization of the small and medium size enterprise (SME) as a competitive strategy, the pros (benefits) and cons (risks) of going international, and decision-making applications related to SME's and their international expansion. Here, you will find numerous sources of information and analytical tools useful in assessing the benefits, costs, and risks of international expansion as well as market research in its two main formats: marketing-related expansion and manufacturing-related expansion. Furthermore, this book will examine the U.S. market, its macroeconomic performance, business potential and attractiveness in the global marketplace, and multiple global rankings in contrast to comparator countries. Part One includes extensive factual information on the costs and risks of starting and doing business in the United States as well as analytical tools and factual illustrations in industry analysis and regional analysis at the state and municipal levels. The first part closes with an in-depth look at the environment, trends, and dynamics of the small business and entrepreneurship as well as the business start-up logistics in the United States.

In Part Two (Chapters 3 and 4), we introduce the 21st century marketer's toolbox and cover several comprehensive and important methods, tools, and frameworks developed to help you understand the challenges and opportunities facing foreign firms seeking to enter the U.S. market. That said, we focus our content in Part Two primarily on B2C companies that once were small but have since grown through U.S. market expansion by fighting for attention and market penetration, establishing a unique point of difference, and winning market share. Moreover, it is our belief that what holds true for B2C firms seeking U.S. market entry also holds true for B2B and B2G firms as well.

In Chapter 3, we discuss important considerations for planning and executing a successful market entry strategy in the United States. The fundamental principles and ideas contained in this chapter are critical for businesses and organizations exploring expansion, in large part because of their flexibility and adaptability in helping to solve marketing challenges for any size and type (e.g., product- or service-based business) of business, including B2C, B2B, and even B2G businesses. The key points of discussion in Chapter 3 include understanding the dynamics driving consumer behavior change, together with strategies and tactics to help the SME break into the U.S. market and stand out with unique points of differentiation; understanding the diverse and complex American consumer and landscape through the lenses of generational cohorts, geography, and ethnicity; and analytical tools such as the 4Cs, SWOT analysis, and research techniques and resources that can help SMEs to better understand market entry opportunities within the United States.

In Chapter 4, we examine the importance of developing and building a strong and differentiated brand; the development of the marketing mix, or the 4Ps (product, promotion, place, and price), and how it forms your brand's foundation and overall value proposition; and the process of measuring your performance over time, including the role of testing, learning, and optimization (what is referred to as marketing analytics), to help businesses improve and maximize their marketing mix strategy and execution.

Overall, successful market development and entry takes significant research, thought, planning, creativity, commitment, and persistence. Knowing this, and before entering any new market, consider the following four questions:

1. Does the new market offer attractive growth potential? What are the risks? What are the biggest challenges that you face?
2. Are you prepared to commit the necessary time and resources? Expect and anticipate challenges and setbacks along the way.
3. Does your current product or service offering allow for product, message, distribution, and/or pricing flexibility and adaptation in order to meet the needs of this new market?
4. Will you be able to defend and maintain your competitive advantage and/or establish unique points of differentiation in the new market? Do you fully understand what and who (e.g., your competition and consumers) represent this new market?

More specifically, as you develop and execute your international expansion plans, it is important to keep in mind the following priorities that impact the balance of strategic benefits, costs, and risks:

- Is the contemplated expansion a good strategic fit with your company's background, organizational culture, and existing strategic mission?
- Does it enhance the company's strategic strengths and/or mitigate its weaknesses?
- Are there sufficient internal and/or external resources available for expansion?
- What are the short-term and long-term business benefits, costs, and risks associated with expansion? How do they balance against each other in the overall context? Do the benefits outweigh the costs and risks in the case of action versus no action?
- Which countries, markets, or global regions should be prioritized for entry?
- What is the best entry mode/strategy for international expansion?
- Should the company expand early or late?
- Should the expansion be pursued on a small or large scale?

CHAPTER 1

Internationalization of the Small and Medium Size Enterprise

Why Go International?

America is a land of wonders, in which everything is in constant motion and every change seems an improvement.
—Alexis de Tocqueville (1805–1859), a French diplomat, political scientist, and historian

---

Main points in this chapter
- Internationalization of the small and medium size enterprise as a competitive strategy
- Pros and cons of going international
- Applications on SMEs international expansion

Internationalization of the Small and Medium Size Enterprise as a Competitive Strategy

Arguably, the economic mission of a business enterprise is wealth creation for its owners or shareholders. In a broader context this includes job creation, company employee well-being, community/regional development, and other areas of economic and noneconomic nature. There are differences between the missions of for-profit and non-for-profit organizations. In an increasingly competitive world, companies pursue their economic missions and goals by striving for maximization of profit, cost efficiency, return on investment, and a pursuit of other economic priorities.

Globalization vastly expands geographic, political, and socioeconomic boundaries, creating business opportunities for big corporations, small and medium size enterprises (SMEs), and individual entrepreneurs. By the same token, globalization also removes or mitigates obstacles, layers of protection, and political, ideological, and economic constraints associated with government restrictions, distances, language, cultural, logistical, and other cross-country differences near and far away. The forces of globalization level the playing field across nations and industries and exert competitive pressures on companies whether they position themselves domestically or internationally.[1] These forces facilitate internationalization under which business enterprises are in a powerful way lured and/or forced to think and act internationally in search of new opportunities or just to escape competitive pressures at home. Companies and individuals that are absent or slow in embracing this process may miss the crest of the wave of opportunity or suffer strategic defeat in the evolving global competitive field. The advent of the Internet and electronic media enables SMEs to explore the fast-evolving international business landscape and engage in commerce in a cost-efficient manner, often without physically leaving domestic turf.

---

[1] There are plentiful examples illustrating how proliferation of global e-commerce together with advances in transportation and communications have changed the business landscape across industries. The advent of the Internet unleashed tides of creative destruction, wiping out print newspapers, books, and magazines and upending the whole publishing industry. Now bloggers and electronic publishers successfully infringe into these traditional oligopolistic print markets. Amazon and Alibaba have squeezed big name retailers and put out of business numerous shopping malls. For instance, the "baseball hat" or "sneakers" keyword searches on Amazon generate more than 10,000 products each, each visibly displayed and competitively priced: Even the largest department chains like Macy's or sporting goods stores like Big 5 cannot compete with this variety and prices. UPS, FedEx, DHL, and other global shipping companies with their remarkable cost efficiency, precision, and speedy delivery (drone shipments are on the way) backed by real-time order tracing systems have made thousands of small neighborhood mom and pop stores across the United States unable to stay afloat and thus lose ground in this uphill competitive battle. Landline telephone service providers and cable TV operators are being undermined by global giants such as Google, Skype, Facebook, Netflix, and Amazon (the latter is aggressively expanding from retail to the areas of telecommunications and entertainment).

Unless SMEs' decision to go international is political, personal, or emotional (while business decisions are supposed to have a rationale, rationality always coexists with irrational aspects of human nature[2]), it is fundamentally driven by business logic. Under this logic, the scale and forms of SMEs' international business engagement depend on many conditions determined by the company background, current strategic position and operational situation, strategic mission and vision for the future, and personalities among the top leaders. Altogether these characteristics translate into internal strengths and weaknesses. A decision to go international is also determined by the current state, drivers, and future trends in SMEs' external business environment and market forces prevalent in the targeted global region, nation, province, or the entire industry where the enterprise operates. From the company's pragmatic standpoint, these external factors and dynamics in their entirety constitute strategic business opportunities and threats. SMEs' retrospective background and developments determine their current business performance, profile, and strategic posture. Current dynamics constitute a foundation shaping SMEs' future dynamics, developments, and growth.

Although it is conceivable for a business enterprise with a global outreach to simultaneously participate in both international manufacturing and international marketing, companies typically limit their foreign involvement as either a manufacturer or marketer. Participating in both of these typically involves high start-up costs, extraordinary capital commitment, ample financial resources or access to financial borrowing, elevated risks, and strong expertise in the host country. Those are challenges formidable even for large corporations, let alone SMEs.

---

[2]Rationality in actual business decision making is limited by the information managers or entrepreneurs have available, their cognitive limitations, and the finite time under which they have to make a decision. Additionally, as human beings, managers or entrepreneurs in their decisions are impacted by their demographics (e.g., age, gender), race and ethnic affiliation, individual psychological traits (e.g., type A versus type B, introvert versus extravert), organizational politics, micro-group dynamics and macro-organizational culture, personal emotions, likes and dislikes, etc. All together that infuses a dose of irrationality in decision making. Besides individual irrationality and personal cultural preferences (travel, history, climate, etc.), international business decisions are often influenced by family relations, religion, social groups, ideology, and other noneconomic impacts.

Pros and Cons of Going International

A decision to go international or stay domestic involves a comparative analysis of operational, tactical, and strategic benefits, costs, and risks as well as their trade-offs in the action versus no action context. Assuming the economic mission of a business enterprise as wealth creation, we argue that in contemplating their business steps, SMEs act in the interest of maximizing their strategic benefits, minimizing/optimizing costs, and moderating risks. SMEs aiming to go international can gain immediate business benefits such as market expansion, global brand recognition, or secondary (but still critical!) advantages in the economies of scale over smaller rivals. At the same time a company expanding internationally must endure additional costs caused by product adaptation specific to foreign markets, labeling, promotion, and extra personnel designated for new markets. To act, or not to act internationally? Although inaction may often seem an attractive option, doing nothing may result in missed opportunities and loss of competitiveness in the ever changing business landscape and be fraught with its own costs and risks.

Strategic Benefits

Strategic benefits that for-profit companies aim to achieve in their international expansion differ, depending on whether this expansion pursues *marketing* or *manufacturing* in foreign destinations. In general, *marketing-related* international expansion (typically through exporting) gravitates toward countries with a high GDP/capita and a large population, which translate into higher economic gains from business. In this rationale, a high GDP/capita signifies strong spending power, while a large population signifies a sizeable consumer/customer base. Other conditions prompting SMEs in their export-based international expansion may include geographic proximity of the host (foreign) country to their home country, strong market perception of the product in the host, and cultural closeness between the host and the home country. In contrast, *manufacturing-related* international expansion often strives for strategic efficiency through utilization of cheap local factors of production—labor, minerals, energy, land, etc.—in a host country (Carraher and Welsh, 2017).

More specifically, overseas expansion can bring potential *strategic benefits* stemming from the company's international outreach and scale. These include

- increasing market share, sales, and profits;
- advancing corporate competitiveness and brand;
- gaining access to cheap factors of production and resources (primary extracted mineral resources, labor, capital, energy, etc.);
- diversifying geographically and reducing dependence on existing markets;
- taking advantage of geographic proximity to important global markets when product shipping costs from the manufacturing site to the market are prohibitively high;
- extending sales potential of existing product line by expanding the marketing life cycle overseas;
- exploiting existing corporate technology characterized by *short shelf life,* intellectual property, proprietary know-how, or managerial core competencies as competitive advantages and softening seasonal market fluctuations;
- mitigating temporary excessive production capacity that is hard to realize domestically;
- gathering intelligence about foreign competition by probing their defenses through overseas offenses;
- escaping intensity of domestic competition;
- sharpening competitive edge by engaging in global competition;
- escaping tight domestic business regulations, high taxes, or bad corporate image (an increasingly challenging task under the fast-evolving global electronic media);
- taking competitive advantage of the economy on scale, and others.

Along with a wide availability of commercial research databases[3] specific to companies, industries, and countries, there are electronic sources

---

[3]To name a few: ABI/INFORM (features thousands of full-text journals, dissertations, working papers, key business and economics periodicals including country-and industry-focused reports; its international coverage provides a picture of companies and business trends around the world); Academic Search Complete (a

available for free public access that can be easily engaged as a starting point in international business research. One of them is the globalEDGE portal (2017), a mega depository containing research information and analytical and decision-making tools for international business. For example, globalEDGE's annual market potential index[4] (MPI) 2017 provides global rankings for 97 countries worldwide categorized under eight criteria: market size, market intensity, market growth rate, market consumption capacity, commercial infrastructure, market receptivity, economic freedom, country risk, and overall score. Table 1.1 provides a fragment from MPI 2017 comparing market potential across the BRICS (Brazil, Russia, India, China and South Africa) countries. Depending on the specific goal

---

multidisciplinary full-text database, with more than 8,500 full-text periodicals); AdForum.com (focused on the global advertising industry and provides information on over 20,000 agencies and 70,000 advertisements from around the world); Business Source Complete (incorporates more than 4,300 business periodicals); Economist Intelligence Unit (features country analysis on more than 200 markets, industry trends in six key sectors, and the latest management strategies and best practices); Global Market Information Database (GMID, aka Passport by Euromonitor provides comparative statistics for over 205 countries on economic indicators, health, foreign trade, environment, lifestyle, industrial and agriculture output, communications, and more; also includes marketing data for over 350 consumer products and services); IBISWorld (provides industry-based research reports that analyze the business operating risks and opportunities of over 1,300 U.S. industries); LexisNexis Company Dossier (up-to-date information on 13 million U.S. and international companies, offering comprehensive company reports); Mergent Online (financials details of over 25,000 active and inactive U.S. companies). These and other commercial databases are accessible, with variations, to visitors across university libraries in the United States.

[4]Global as opposed to a national or local approach to marketing has become increasingly important over the years as trends toward internationalization are gaining momentum. Faced with too many choices, marketers have the challenge of determining which international markets to enter and the appropriate marketing strategies for those countries. The purpose of this study is to rank, with a U.S. focus, the market potential of 97 identified countries and to provide guidance to the U.S. companies that plan to expand their markets internationally. While the United States is not included in the rankings, the insights provided by the index are still applicable to companies located in other international markets. Eight dimensions are chosen to represent the market potential of a country on a scale of 1 to 100. The dimensions are measured using various indicators and are weighted in determining their contribution to the overall MPI (globalEDGE, 2017).

Table 1.1 *Market Potential Index (MPI) 2017 of the BRICS countries*

	Overall MPI		Scores on specific MPI criteria (out of 100)							
Country	Rank (out of 97)	Score (out of 100)	Market Size	Market Growth Rate	Market Intensity	Market Consumption Capacity	Commercial Infrastructure	Economic Freedom	Market Receptivity	Country Risk
Brazil	20	33	17	62	48	41	57	50	5	69
China	1	100	100	100	4	97	55	22	8	79
India	7	46	37	76	36	56	14	46	8	64
Russia	15	36	18	71	40	51	80	27	8	64
S. Africa	70	18	5	61	46	1	59	55	9	58

Source: globalEDGE (2017).

7

of foreign expansion, SMEs can rationalize their selection of the best target markets in first approximation by conducting a comparative analysis of the global rankings under one of the eight selection criteria.

In addition to the MPI country index, globalEDGE publishes annual global indexes for 12 industries: advanced manufacturing, aerospace, agriculture, alternative energy, automotive electronics and composites/lightweight materials, biosciences, chemicals, food processing, information technology, land-based products, machinery, and medical devices.[5] As its name suggests, MPI index provides only a general picture, not thorough analytical information sufficient for specific decision making on overseas expansion. Industries vary in their profitability, strategic drivers and constraints, trends, cost structure, and other dynamics; therefore, decisions like this involve gathering business intelligence resulting from comprehensive, specialized international market research and industry- and country-specific consulting assistance.

Major international institutions such as the International Energy Agency (2017), International Monetary Fund (2017), Organization for Economic Co-operation and Development (2017), United Nations Conference on Trade and Development (2017), World Bank (2017), World Trade Organization (2017), and others publish a wide variety of respective country and thematic reports rich in factual and analytical information that can be useful in a background analysis preceding SMEs' international expansion decisions.

The annual Global Competitiveness Report (GCR, 2017)[6] by the Switzerland-based World Economic Forum is another useful analytical tool that can be used for country/market selection designated for international expansion. On the one hand, rich and reasonably concise analytical information presented in this report reflects the state of competitiveness

---

[5]Additionally, globlEDGE also publishes Insights by Industry for 20 distinct industry sectors containing wealth of information for each industry.

[6]Global Competitiveness Report framework available complimentary online incorporates 12 *pillars of competitiveness:* institutions, infrastructure, macroeconomic environment, health and primary education, higher education and training, goods market efficiency, labor market efficiency, financial market development, technological readiness, market size, business sophistication, and innovation. The latest 2017–2018 report covers 137 countries.

across countries worldwide in a comparative perspective, and on the other hand, the better a country's global competitive rankings and the more robust its competitive metrics are, the more attractive it is likely to be from an international business standpoint. More specifically, the country's strong rankings in global competitiveness tend to correlate with its attractiveness as a host (recipient) country for exporting and foreign direct investments. SMEs contemplating international expansion can use the GCR by tailoring its comparative analysis of alternative target countries specific to their specific situation and strategic priorities.

Another useful analytical assessment tool in national global competitiveness is the annual World Competitiveness Yearbook (WCY) by the Switzerland-based International Institute for Management Development (IMD).[7] The basic version of WCY, offering limited information, can be accessed online free of charge. More comprehensive country reports from WCY can be obtained for a fee.

National government agencies tasked with promoting international commerce and foreign investment for their countries are also an excellent source of analytical information and assistance in support of SMEs' international expansion. This analysis and support can be obtained complimentarily or very inexpensively. For example, the U.S. Commercial Service, part of the U.S. Department of Commerce's International Trade Administration, offers companies, particularly SMEs, a full range of expertise in international trade through its export.gov portal (2017). Export. gov offers a vast amount of analytical information that includes annual

---

[7] WCY analyzes and ranks the ability of nations to create and maintain an environment that sustains the competitiveness of enterprises (whether private or state owned). In WCY, this field of research is called *competitiveness of enterprises*. Enterprises operate in a national environment that enhances or hinders their ability to compete domestically or internationally. In WCY, this field of research is called *competitiveness of nations*. The methodology of the WCY divides the national environment into four main factors: economic performance, government efficiency, business efficiency, and infrastructure. In turn, each of these factors is divided into sub-factors. Altogether, WCY features more than 300 analytical criteria. WCY claims the superiority of its rankings over the GCR by the World Economic Forum by covering 300 indicators compared with only 120 indicators in GCR and a much greater reliance on hard data compared with interviews/questionnaires in GCR.

Country Commercial Guides (2017), Export Information by Industry (2017), and National Trade Data and Analysis (2017). The U.S. Commercial Service (2017) provides its support through 108 domestic offices nationwide as well as more than 75 countries across the globe (Where We Are 2017). The International Trade Administration's (2017) services for U.S.-based companies rendered through both domestic and international office include the following standard programs:

- Counseling on Antidumping and Countervailing Duty
- Export Counseling
- Gold Key Matching
- International Buyer Program
- International Company Profile
- International Partner Search
- Market Research
- Platinum Key
- Report a Trade Barrier
- Privacy Shield Certification
- Steel Import Licensing
- Trade Compliant Filing
- Trade Fair Certification
- Trade Leads.

For example, the U.S. Commercial Service Office in Russia (2017) offers trade counseling services in market intelligence, business matchmaking, and commercial diplomacy (Russia is Open for Your Business 2017). One of its popular services, designed to be the most cost effective means for U.S. exporters to enter the important and complex Russian market, is the Gold Key Matching Service (2017). The program features options such as

- appointments (typically four per day) with prescreened Russian firms;
- background and contact information on each potential partner, for example, the size of the company, number of years in business, product or service lines, and capability to provide after-sales service;
- customized market briefing with U.S. Commercial Service staff;

- available market research on the relevant industry sector;
- debriefing with U.S. Commercial staff to discuss results and plan follow-up action and more.

The cost structure for the Gold Key Matching Service is $700 for each SME[8] and $350 per SME for new-to-export companies using this service for the first time (Gold Key Matching Service, 2017).

National agencies tasked with promoting international commerce and foreign investment in economically advanced nations like Australia (Australian Trade and Investment Commission, 2017); Canada (International Trade and Investment, 2017); France (Business France, 2017); Germany (Germany: Trade & Invest, 2017); Japan (Japan External Trade Organization, 2017); Korea (Korea Trade–Investment Promotion Agency, 2017); Spain (Invest in Spain, 2017); and the United Kingdom (Department for International Trade, 2017). Other countries offer similar services that SMEs based in these respective countries should consider in their preparation for international expansion.

Major global management consultancies, such as Bain (2017), Boston Consulting Group Ernst & Young (2017), KPMG (2017), and PricewaterhouseCoopers (2017); and many others analytical centers regularly publish analytical reports on specific countries, industries, and international business themes.

In addition to the print and electronic library resources, entrepreneurs contemplating internationalization should consider engaging consulting assistance and support. Resources include the U.S. Department of Commerce (domestically): www.buyusa.gov/home/us.html, the U.S. Commercial Service (internationally): www.buyusa.gov/home/worldwide_us.html, the American Chamber (AmCham) of Commerce offices overseas and bilateral chambers of commerce (e.g., German American Chambers of Commerce www.gaccsouth.com/en/), foreign government consulates and other agencies in the United States (many countries

---

[8]US Commercial Service defines a small or medium-sized enterprise (SME) as a firm with 500 or fewer employees or self-certified as a small business under SBA regulations. A large company is defined as a firm with more than 500 employees. Subsidiaries will be classified based on the size of the parent company.

have their trade promotion offices in major U.S. cities), and international trade/marketing consultants. Major industries have their professional associations providing consulting services, maintaining information depositories, organizing networking events, and providing other support on international business.

Costs

Costs associated with international expansion vary widely. For example, industries, due to their own technological conditions and economic dynamics, may be labor, capital, land, or energy intensive. The cost of doing business across countries also fluctuates due to the differences in their economic geography and climate, business environment, mineral resource endowment, infrastructure, and operational efficiency. Additionally, it depends on the company's entry strategy and mode of operation. For example, in case of *exporting*, the cargo shipping, tariffs, insurance, and some other items constitute major expenditures on the top of the product manufacturing cost. An overseas *manufacturing* project under the *greenfield* investment or the international joint venture format may involve sizeable long-term financing requirements, home and host country personnel commitment, and a large scale capital asset allocation. Entering an international licensing or franchising agreement is less capital intensive, but may involve considerable legal fees and intellectual property protection expenditures. The costs of overseas expansion are also highly dependent on the company's management and operational efficiency.

The World Bank Group's annual "Doing Business" report can serve as a useful analytical tool for comparative cross-country cost assessment. "Doing Business" measures aspects of business regulation affecting domestic small and medium size firms defined on the basis of standardized case scenarios and located in the largest business city of each economy. In addition, for 11 economies a second city is covered. The latest 2017 "Doing Business" survey covers 11 areas of business regulation across 190 economies. Ten of these areas—starting a business, dealing with construction permits, getting electricity, registering property, getting credit, protecting minority investors, paying taxes, trading across borders, enforcing contracts, and resolving insolvency—are included in the *distance to frontier score* and *ease of doing business ranking.* "Doing Business" also measures features of labor market regulation, which is not included in the afore-mentioned two measures (Doing Business, 2017).

Table 1.2, compiled from the "Doing Business 2017" report, con-trasts the ease/cost of doing business in five countries. Germany, Japan, and the United States are included as leading economies representing the global *triad;* China and Russia are the points of contrast as major global emerging markets. For the sake of illustration, Table 1.2 includes only four criteria from "Doing Business": ease of doing business in gen-eral, protecting minority investors, enforcing contracts, and trading across borders. In fact, the "Doing Business" report contains much more analytical information for each of these areas, which is not included in Table 1.2. As shown in the table, based on the overall rankings in the ease of doing business, the United States emerges as the most attractive country, followed by Germany, Japan, Russia, and China, respectively. Broadening this analysis to include the remaining areas of analysis and data from "Doing Business" as well as supplementing it with industry- and company-specific cost information from other sources will add comprehension and rigor to this cost examination, contributing to more informed and justified decisions on the company's international expansion.

Company-specific cost information is often a secret closely guarded by management and difficult for an outsider to obtain. A partial solution to this problem can be the KPMG biannual "Competitive Alternatives" (2016) report containing comprehensive cost information for interna-tional business locations specific to 10 countries, 19 industries, 28 cost components, and more than 100 cities worldwide. SMEs contemplat-ing foreign manufacturing–driven expansion can better rationalize their decision by comparing and contrasting industry costs across countries and cities. For example, a comparative national cost index for the pro-fessional services sector/international financial services industry is com-puted in the KPMG report as follows: the United States, 100 percent; Mexico, 56.9 percent (44.1 percentage point cost advantage over the United States); Canada, 72.4 percent; the Netherlands, 77.3 percent; Australia, 78.3 percent; Italy, 80.3 percent; Germany, 81.4 percent; France, 82.8 percent; Japan, 85.6 percent; and the United Kingdom,

Table 1.2 Comparative costs of doing business in countries

| | Ease of doing business overall | Protecting minority investors | | Enforcing contracts | | Trading across borders | |
	Rank (out of 190 economies)	Rank (out of 190 economies)	Strength of minority investor protection index (0–10)	Rank (out of 190 economies)	Cost (% of claim)	Rank (out of 190 economies)	Time to import: Documentary compliance (hours)
China	78	123	4.5	5	16.2	96	66
Germany	17	53	6	17	14.4	38	1
Japan,	34	53	6	48	23.4	49	3
Russia	40	53	6	12	16.5	140	43
United States	8	41	6.5	20	30.5	35	8

Source: "Doing Business, 2017."

86.7 percent (Competitive Alternatives, 2016). Thus, from the cost minimization perspective for the international financial services industry, Mexico and Canada present the most attractive options.[9]

Risks

Risks are an integral part of domestic and international business. International business risks tend to be more complex and potent compared with domestic risks due to greater geographic distances, cross-country variations in political–economic and legal systems, divergences in judiciary systems, cultural discrepancies, language and communication barriers, and chance events such as natural disasters, wars, political upheavals, financial–economic crises, and sudden changes in the government. Due to their nature and complexity, many risks in international business are hard to predict and harder yet to avoid.

While business risks cannot be eliminated completely, they can be mitigated through preliminary background research, intelligence gathering, due diligence, country selection grounded in low risks, entry strategy selection characterized by lowest risks, finding the right partners and fostering their trust and commitment, establishing transparent and efficient operating procedures, engaging in foreign currency exchange hedging, and/or building lasting personal relations.

General information on country risk analysis and assessment can be obtained from numerous commercial electronic databases—Business Source Complete, LexisNexis, Business Insights Global, GMID/Euromonitor/Passport, ABI/INFORM, to name a few. More specific risk assessment information and useful financial analysis related to risks can be obtained from such publications as the *Almanac of Business and Industrial Financial Ratios, Handbook of Industry Profiles,* and *Standard & Poor's Industry Surveys.* Complimentary access to these and other databases can be obtained through university and public libraries as well as other channels.

A good first step in international business risk assessment may lie in analyzing risk profiles across countries and industries contained in

---

[9]In addition to the cost of doing business per se, the comparative national cost index values for different countries are affected by the going currency exchange rates.

publications and other reports by large insurance companies serving a global corporate clientele. These insurance service providers offer country risk assessment on the basis of sophisticated statistical models and comprehensive macroeconomic databases.

The globalEDGE (2017) database offers access to country risk information summaries based on the Coface Group[10] data. More comprehensive risk assessment information on the country and economic sector level can be obtained directly from the company site (Coface, 2017). Another source of risk assessment information is the Belgium-based Credendo Group,[11] a global insurer (Credendo, 2017). The U.S.-based A.M. Best Rating Services[12] (2017) provides risk assessment profiles for 107 countries worldwide.

As an example, Figures 1.1 through 1.4 present country risk assessment profiles for the United States by Coface, Credendo, and A.M. Best, respectively. As seen from these charts, economic, political, financial, and trade-related risks in the United States are at their lowest, except for a slightly elevated level of economic risks. Contrasting America's risks with Germany and Japan reveals similarly low levels of risks: Germany's risks are slightly lower and Japan's are slightly higher compared with those of the United States in all the three assessments. However, for China and Russia, the world's major emerging markets, the situation is different: Their risk level (China's somewhat lower compared with Russia's) is notably higher compared with that of Germany, Japan, and the United States. This analysis sends a clear message to a risk averse SME expanding internationally in its selection of the foreign target market.

---

[10]The French-based Coface Group is an insurance firm with direct presence in 66 countries and guarantees delivered in nearly 200 countries.

[11]Credendo is fourth largest European credit insurance group active in all segments of trade credit and political risk insurance, providing a range of products that cover risks in more than 200 countries worldwide.

[12]A.M. Best (founded in 1899) issues insurance ratings on approximately 3,400 companies and 16,000 insurance companies globally in more than 90 countries worldwide.

POPULATION
321,601 MILLION

GDP PER CAPITA
56 084 US$

A2
COUNTRY RISK
ASSESSMENT

A1
BUSINESS
CLIMATE

Strengths	**Weaknesses**
• Flexibility in the labor market	• Low employment rate
• Full employment is also one of the objectives of the Federal Reserve	• Households' limited geographic flexibility
• Predominant role of the dollar in the global economy	• Polarization of political landscape
• Nearly 60% of public debt held by residents	• Lower fertility rate
• Growing energy self-sufficiency	• Obsolescence of many infrastructures

Figure 1.1 The United States: risk assessment profile by Coface

Source: Coface, 2017.

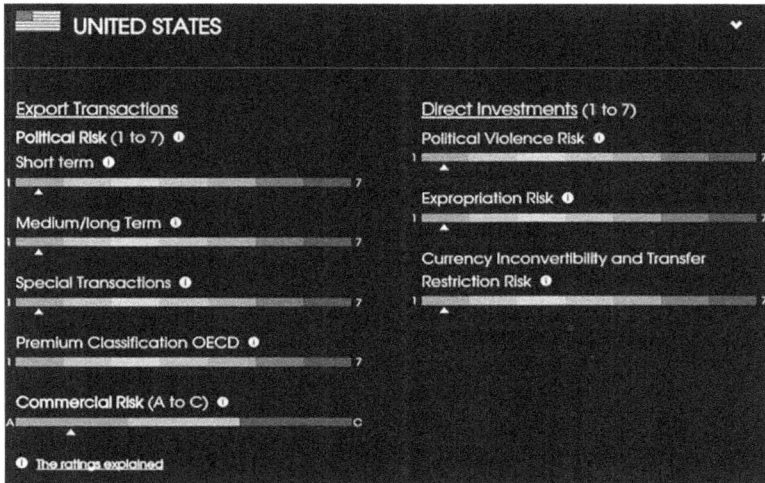

UNITED STATES

Export Transactions

Political Risk (1 to 7) ❶
Short term ❶

Medium/long Term ❶

Special Transactions ❶

Premium Classification OECD ❶

Commercial Risk (A to C) ❶

❶ The ratings explained

Direct Investments (1 to 7)

Political Violence Risk ❶

Expropriation Risk ❶

Currency Inconvertibility and Transfer
Restriction Risk ❶

Note: Level I on the 7-point scale signifies the lowest risk, level 7 signifies the highest risk.
Level A in commercial risks signifies the lowest risk, level C signifies the highest risk.

Figure 1.2 The United States: risk assessment profile by Credendo

Source: Credendo, 2017.

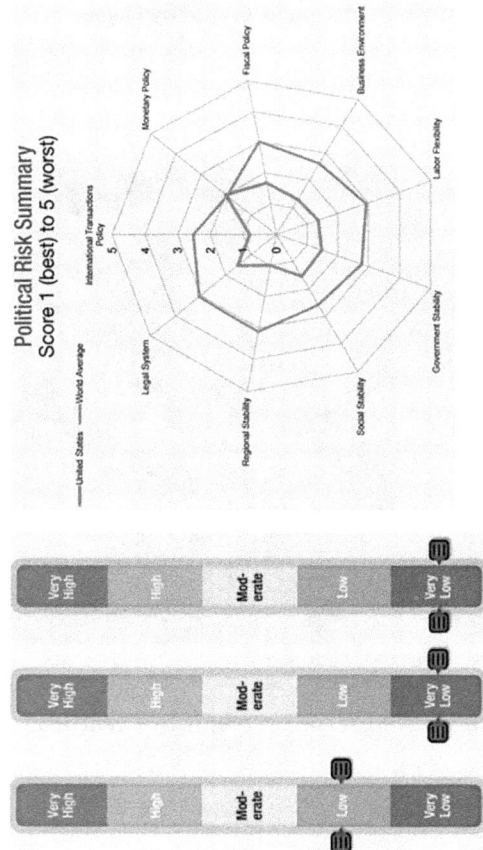

Political Risk Summary
Score 1 (best) to 5 (worst)

—— United States ——— World Average

- The Country Risk Tier (CRT) reflects A.M. Best's assessment of three categories of risk: Economic, Political and Financial System Risk.
- The U.S. is a CRT-1 country with very low or low levels of economic, political and financial system risk. Gross domestic product (GPD) growth has been moderate at rate of 2.4% in 2015 and an expected 2.4% in 2016. Medium term growth is expected to be between 2.0% and 2.5%. Global uncertainty and low levels of business investment have been headwinds for the U.S. economy.
- Economic performance in the region echoes that of the U.S., the dominate economy. U.S. consumer spending, which accounts for approximately 70% of the economy, has been resilient due to low levels of unemployment, gains in disposable incomes and higher asset prices.

Country Risk Tier 5 (CRT-5)
Very High Level of Country Risk

Country Risk Tier 4 (CRT-4)
High Level of Country Risk

Country Risk Tier 3 (CRT-3)
Moderate Level of Country Risk

Country Risk Tier 2 (CRT-2)
Low Level of Country Risk

Figure 1.3 The United States: risk assessment profile by A.M. Best

Source: A.M. Best, 2016.

Economic Risk: Low	Political Risk: Very Low	Financial System Risk: Very Low
• The U.S. economy is the largest and most advanced in the world, with GDP of more than 18.2 trillion USD at the end of Q1 2016. • Economic growth continues to be stable, driven by personal consumption and steady job creation. Healthy job creation translated into higher personal disposable income, supporting household spending. • The housing market continues to recover due to low interest rates, increasing demand, higher rental prices, improving credit conditions and rising real estate prices. • The federal funds rate forecast at the beginning of 2016 largely predicted at least one interest rate hike in 2016, as the Federal Reserve attempts to normalize monetary policy from the current historically low interest rates.	• The U.S. has a stable democratic political system and a strong legal system. Political infighting has led to significant dysfunction and inaction in Washington in recent years. • The House and Senate are currently controlled by the Republican party. Infighting in the party and posturing ahead of the presidential election will limit effective policy making. • The U.S. has seen a rise in political populism as voters increasingly view government and corporate interests as aligned. National security, immigration, race relations, and income inequality will continue to dominate much of U.S. politics heading into the Presidential election of 2016. • Uncertainty over the 2016 presidential election could lead to uncertainty over international relations and the potential for trade deals in the near future.	• Insurance regulation in the US is decentralized and handled on a state by-state basis. However, recent legislative changes tasked the Federal Reserve with providing additional oversight on some of the largest U.S.-based companies. • As of 2010, the Federal Insurance Office, under the Department of the Treasury, is responsible for monitoring the insurance industry for regulatory gaps, systemic risk, and international issues. • The financial system is stable with deep and liquid markets and well capitalized firms. • In June 2016, the Federal Reserve released the results of its Dodd-Frank Act Stress Tests on the largest banks in the United States. Almost all of these banks passed the stress tests, which are performed in ensure adequate levels of capitalization.

Figure 1.4 **The United States Risk Assessment profile by A.M. Best**

Source: A.M. Best, 2016.

Contemplating International Expansion: Analytical Tools, Sources of Assistance, and Applications

Which Countries, Markets, or Global Regions should SMEs Target as a Priority?

There are more than 200 sovereign nations around the world, including 193 members of the United Nations (United Nations, 2017). From a business opportunity standpoint, each of these countries is characterized by its own unique geographic and political–economic conditions, laws and regulatory environment, physical and business infrastructure, cultural customs, and business practices thus constituting different business potential and attractiveness for an SME. Under resource constraints, SMEs exploiting this opportunity through international expansion should carefully prioritize country selection in pursuit of the optimal balance in strategic benefits, costs, and risks. Mistakes in country selection may prove costly, and simultaneous expansion to multiple countries may be a bad decision—it stretches SMEs' limited resources thin and can result in failure due to the costs, risks, and complexity involved in multiple locations (A Basic Guide to Exporting 2016).

Dissimilarities in drivers and dynamics between the marketing-related and manufacturing-related overseas expansion alternatives require different approaches for selecting target countries in these cases. A marketing-driven expansion tends to be simpler, less costly, and less risky than a manufacturing-driven expansion. A typical export transaction involves just logistics of goods and services characterized by shorter time frames, smaller financial commitments, and limited risks. In contrast, manufacturing-driven expansion may involve a sizeable financial commitment for foreign direct investment; higher costs, liabilities, and risks; and complex logistics and management issues associated with expansion and operations in a host country.

There is a wide range of available manuals, tutorials, and other sources of information and assistance on exporting—some of them mentioned earlier in this chapter. In the interest of time and cost efficiency, companies contemplating their export-related international expansion may apply a *one stop shop* approach and start their exploration by tapping the most comprehensive sources enabling background research. A case in point is the International Trade Compliance Institute (2017) database that offers complimentary access to a wide range of resources on international trade.

Among them is the Four Stages in Export Development (2017) framework created by Maurice Kogon (Figure 1.5). The framework outlines and integrates key stages (Build Export Capacity, Develop Export Markets, Make Sales/Get Paid, and Deliver the Goods) in the holistic export development process and outlines the necessary steps for each stage.

Another useful source of information and analytical tool is the Step-by-Step Approach to Market Research (2017). The four-pronged step-by-step procedure by export.gov lists key analytical and decision making steps as well as sources of assistance enabling an exporting SME to identify and strategically explore overseas target markets in the right order of priority.

Step-by-Step Approach to Market Research[13]

Step 1: Find Potential Markets

- Obtain trade statistics that indicate which countries import your type(s) of products.
- Perform a thorough review of the available market research reports in the country (ies) and industries in question to determine market openness, common practices, tariffs and taxes, distribution channels, and other important considerations.
- Identify 5 to 10 large and fast-growing markets for the firm's product(s). Analyze them over the past three to five years for market growth in good and bad times.
- Identify some smaller but fast-emerging markets where there may be fewer competitors.
- Target three to five of the most statistically promising markets for further assessment. Consult with the U.S. Export Assistance Center near you.

Step 2: Assess Targeted Markets

- Examine consumption and production of competitive products as well as overall demographic and economic trends in the target country.

---

[13]By using this link https://www.export.gov/article?id=Step-by-Step-Guide and clicking on embedded words the user is directed to sources of market research information and assistance along the process.

Stage 1 →	Stage 2 →	Stage 3 →	Stage 4
Build Export Capacity →	Develop Export Markets →	Make Sales / Get Paid →	Deliver the Goods →

Improve Competitiveness
Situation analysis / SWOTT
Solidify fundamentals
Production processes
• Business practices
• Operating/working capital
	Identify Best Markets
	Market research / analysis
	• Select target markets
	• Assess target markets
	  • Competition
	  • Market segments
	  • Market conditions / barriers
		Close the Deal
		Respond to inquiries
		Quote prices (INCOTERMS)
		Negotiate sales terms
			Regulatory Compliance
			U.S regulatory compliance
			Foreign regulatory compliance

Develop Export Readiness Assess export potential & readiness Enhance export potential & readiness • Export advice & counseling • Export training & education	**Develop Entry Strategies** Market strategy planning • Distribution / pricing / promotion • Adaptation / localization • Implementation/action plan • Resource / budget plan	**Finance Sales/Get Paid** Payment methods/services • Pre-export financing • Transaction financing • Export credit insurance • Factoring / forfaiting Payment Sources/Aids • Commercial banks • Export-Import Bank • Factors / forfaiters	**Documentary Compliance** U.S documentary compliance Foreign documentary compliance
Get/Use Export Help Trade assistance network • DOC / US&FCS, USDA / FAS • State / local ITACs • Chambers / Associations / WTCs Trade assistance resources • Partner programs / services • Partner client databases • Internet trade sites	**Implement Entry Strategies** Find partners (buyers/distributors) • Trade leads • International partner searches • Screen/select partners Promote export sales • Broadcast promotion • Targeted promotion Market promotion financing		**Transport the Goods** Manage the supply chain Prepare goods for delivery Book cargo / ship the goods

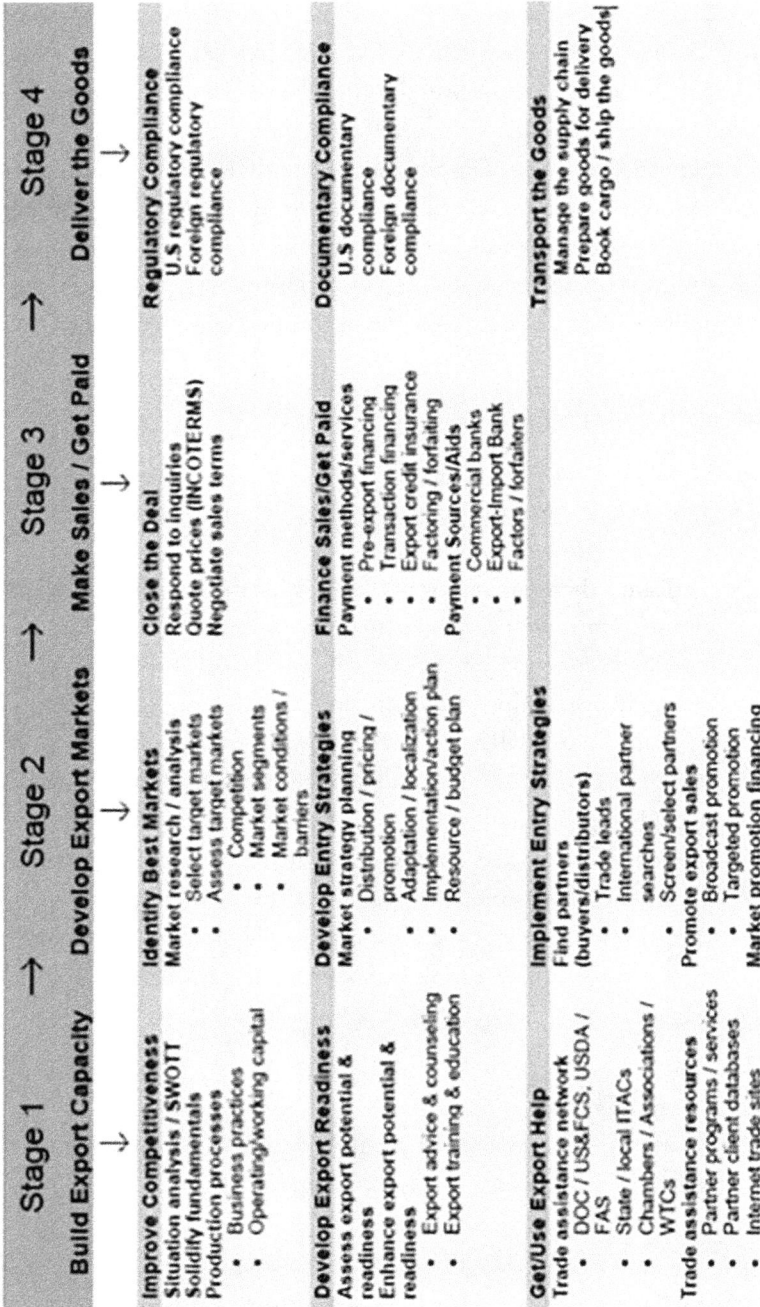

Figure 1.5 Four stages in export development

Source: International Trade Compliance Institute, 2017.

- Ascertain the sources of competition, including the extent of domestic industry production and the major foreign countries the firm would compete against.
- Analyze factors affecting marketing and use of the product in each market, such as end-user sectors, channels of distribution, cultural idiosyncrasies, and business practices.
- Identify any foreign barriers (tariff or nontariff) for the product being imported into the country and identify any U.S. export licenses you may need.
- Identify U.S. or foreign incentives to promote exporting of your product or service.
- Determine whether your product is price competitive after you've figured in packaging, shipping, marketing, sales commissions, taxes and tariffs, and other associated costs. See pricing considerations.

Step 3: Draw Conclusions

If the company is new to exporting, it is probably a good idea to target only two or three markets initially. A local US Export Assistance Center can provide valuable insight into your *optimal* market opportunities.

Step 4: Test Demand

There are a number of low-cost online and offline services that can help new exporters gauge foreign market interest and collect overseas inquiries:

- Catalog Exhibitions
- Foreign Partner Matching and Trade Lead Services

A deployment of the Step-by-Step Market Research framework in an export-driven international market research can be supplemented by multiple analytical and decision-making tools for exporters. For example, the reader can complimentary access the extensive Los Angeles Regional Export Council (2017) database.

Selecting a target country for a manufacturing-driven international expansion, whether it is a greenfield foreign investment or an international acquisition, can be achieved through an exploration of business opportunities involving foreign investment and a comparative cross-country analysis of investment climate. Both of these analyses can be accomplished and rationalized by applying the benefit–cost–risk assessment framework. Due to the high complexity and vast variety of information resources, we limit our discussion by just a few sources.

- Annual Country Commercial Guides (2017) and information on country portals by the U.S. Commercial Service[14] (International Offices 2017) are a must read for an SME contemplating foreign expansion. Chapter 4 of a Country Commercial Guide identifies country-specific leading sectors for U.S. exports and investment and provides a vital background information—a good starting point. Country Commercial Guides and country portals also offer a wide range of useful information and assistance on doing business in specific countries worldwide.
- Country information resources in the globalEDGE (2017) portal are organized into the following sections: Introduction, History, Government, Economy, Statistics, Trade Statistics, Culture, Risk, Corporations, Indices, Resources, U.S. Trade Resources, and Memo. Depending on the time, scope, and depth of analysis, the approach can vary from engaging short sections such as Memo or Introduction to a wider format including specialized sections and supplementary resources. The Indices section enables the user to generate the country's global rankings across more than a dozen parameters, thus providing a comparative profile and revealing the level of its attractiveness for business.
- Investment Climate Statements (2017) published annually by the U.S. Department of State provide country- and economy-specific information and assessments on investment-related laws and other important factors. The statements are designed to provide detailed information on the strengths and weaknesses and recent trends in each economy's environment for foreign investment. This information,

---

[14]Obviously, U.S. Department of Commerce and U.S. Foreign Commercial Service tailor their analysis, reports, and services toward American companies. Mentioned earlier in this chapter are several other countries whose trade promotion agencies provide similar support for citizens and companies of their respective jurisdictions.

spanning 170 foreign markets, can assist U.S. companies to make informed decisions regarding investment in foreign markets. The Investment Climate Statements include examples of countries and economies expanding openness to foreign investment and investor protections as well as challenges and barriers that may exist. Topics covered for each country and economy include openness to investment, legal and regulatory systems, dispute resolution, intellectual property rights, transparency, performance requirements, the role of state-owned enterprises, responsible business conduct, and corruption, among others.

• The earlier mentioned "Competitive Alternatives" biannual report by KPMG provides company-level comparative information on cost efficiency across numerous countries, cities, and industries worldwide.

What is the Best Entry Mode/Strategy Overseas?

After the SME has identified a target country for expansion it should consider selecting an entry mode/strategy that ensures the best (optimal) balance of strategic benefits, costs, and risks.[15] Besides economic considerations such as profitability, cost efficiency, or market share, the choice of entry mode, as applicable, should ensure a sound management and intellectual property protection. The latter is particularly critical for internationally

---

[15]It is not uncommon for SMEs and large corporations to experience conflicts in prioritizing their international and domestic strategic decisions. Depending on the company core competencies, internal strategic strengths and weaknesses, external market opportunities and threats, competitive forces in the SME's target markets, and other factors, at various stages of growth it may be more important to pursue strategic benefits in the aggressive expansion and brand building while keeping the cost containment as a secondary priority. Amazon is a case in point: Although the company was founded in 1994, almost a quarter of century ago, it became profitable relatively recently, after many years of losing money. However, this approach has enabled Amazon to become the brand and market leader in global electronic commerce with a dominant market share in the United States that has transformed the whole industry and put many traditional retailers out of business or on the defensive. Under the different interplay of market forces and the SME's priorities, a pursuit of strategic opportunities can be sacrificed with the cost cutting and/or risk avoidance shifting toward the forefront to become paramount priorities.

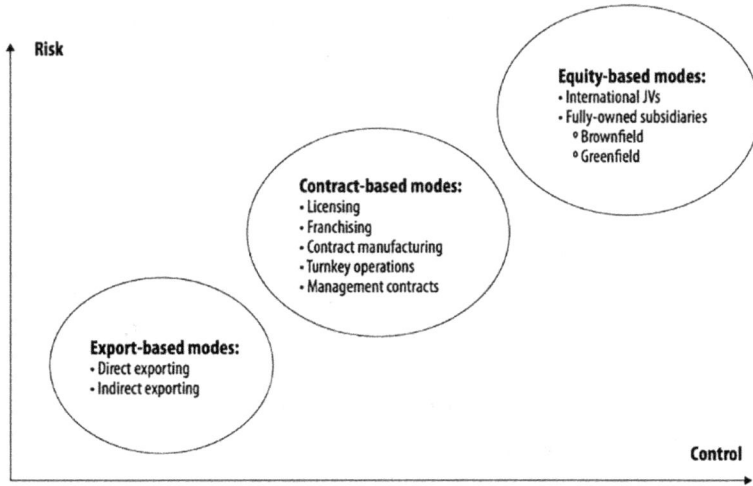

Figure 1.6 International entry modes

Source: Global Entrepreneurship, 2017.

operating companies whose competitive advantages lie in technologically sensitive products, services, or processes. The most common international entry modes include direct and indirect exporting/importing, international licensing and franchising, international turnkey projects, wholly owned subsidiaries in the form of international greenfield investment and acquisition, joint ventures, and various strategic alliances. Each of these alternative entry modes is characterized by its own pros, cons, situational applicability, and constraints. Figures 1.6 and 1.7 summarize some of these entry modes and their comparative advantages and disadvantages.

Applications on SME's International Expansion

The remaining part of this chapter contains an integrative exercise in application related to SME internationalization. The application integrates main aspects and key components of a background research involved in an SME internationalization decision: -company analysis (SWOT format); country selection under comparative assessment of strategic benefits, costs, and risks; company-level export-readiness assessment; and export-driven market research. Depending on the purpose of this practical application (an actual international business research or an educational

MODE OF ENTRY	ADVANTAGES	DISADVANTAGES
Exporting	low risk Easy market entry or exit Gain local market knowledge Bypass FDI restrictions	Tariffs and quotas Transportation costs Possible distributor relationship issues

Licensing	low risk
	Fast market access
	Bypass regulations and tariffs
	Gain local market knowledge
		less control over market and
		   revenues
		Intellectual property concerns
		Potential problems with licensees/
		   future competitors

Franchising	low financial risk
	Bypass regulations and tariffs
	Keep more control
	Gain local market knowledge
		less control over market and
		   revenues
		Some loss of control over operations
		Potential franchisee relationship
		   issues

Contract manufacturing	low financial risk
	Save on manufacturing costs
	Flexibility of short term
	   commitment
	Emphasis on Marketing/sales
		less control over operations
		less knowledge about local market
		Potential damage to brand/finances
		   if human rights issues arise

Management contracts	Insider access to market Emphasis on firm's expertise low financial risk	Limited profits and market access Potential copyright and intellectual property issues

Turnkey operations	Access to FDI-unfriendly
	   markets
	No long term operational risks
	Emphasis on firm's expertise
		Some financial risk
		Potential issues with partners/
		   infrastructure/labor / profit
		   repatriation

Joint ventures	Insider access to market
	High profit potential
	More control over operations
	Shared risks
	Gain knowledge from
	   partner(s)
		High investment of resources
		Potential issues between partners
		   over control/contributions/goals,
		   etc.
		More management levels
		Potential intellectual property
		   issues

Fully owned subsidiaries	Full market access/acceptance
	Full control over operations/
	   profits
	Bypass tariffs
	Diversify operations
		High financial/resources investment
		High political and environmental
		   risks
		Potential profits repatriation issues
		More management levels

Figure 1.7 Advantages and disadvantages of international modes of entry

Source: Global Entrepreneurship, 2017.

exercise), time allocation, and other organizational and logistical conditions, it may include the exercise in its entirety or just selected steps.

Four-Step Application: Strategic Research for SME's Internationalization

Step 1: SME SWOT Analysis

- An SME is contemplating international expansion (entry into foreign market).
  - Alternatively, the reader can select an export-oriented SME advertising its product at http://exusa.thinkglobal.us/ (Export USA 2017).
- Conduct SWOT (strengths, weaknesses, opportunities, and threats) analysis for the SME.
- Based on the SWOT analysis, summarize the SME's specific pros and cons of going international and rationalize your recommendation on whether the SME should go international or expand its existing international operations.

Step 2: Country Selection: Comparative Assessment of Strategic Benefits, Costs, and Risks

- Benefits: Go to http://globaledge.msu.edu/knowledge-tools/mpi (globalEDGE 2017). Review the latest available MPI. Based on the SWOT analysis and recommendations from Step 1, select three MPI criteria[16] (prioritize as appropriate) reflecting county attractiveness from the SME's international expansion perspective. Using these criteria as a selection tool, identify two most attractive (target) countries from the BRICS list.[17] Go to http://globaledge .msu.edu/global-insights/by/country (globalEDGE 2017). Compare

---

[16]The number of criteria and the number of potential target countries can be expanded as appropriate, depending on specific goals and practical needs.

[17]Germany, Japan, the United States, and other advanced economies are not covered by the MPI, thus limiting analysis to 97 developing and emerging markets only.

and contrast global indices for the two best target BRICS locations in terms of their attractiveness for the SME's business.

- Costs: Go to http://www.doingbusiness.org/ ("Doing Business 2017"). Click on the GEt alL DATA link in the upper right corner. In *Select Economy* F0E0 SHOW ALL F0E0 check the boxes for your two target locations/countries; in *Choose Topics* F0E0 check the boxes for Protecting Minority Investors, Enforcing Contracts, and Trading across Borders[18]; In *Which Data Years Do You Wish to Display?* F0E0 check a box for the latest available "Doing Business" report or the one for a specific year of your interest. Click on the CREATE REPORT button on the right-hand side.
- Risks: Go to https://www.credendo.com/country_risk (Credendo. 2017). Identify strategic risks of doing business in two target locations by clicking on these countries' names in the scroll-down window. Contrast and compare strategic risks of doing business for the two target locations. If necessary, conduct country risk assessment by using alternative Coface (2017) and/or A.M. Best (2016) databases.

Based on your comparative assessment of strategic benefits, costs, and risks, evaluate country attractiveness for the SME's business?

Step 3: Company-level Export-Readiness Assessment

- Go to http://www.tradecomplianceinstitute.org/ERAS/eras_index .php (Trade Compliance Institute, 2017). Complete the SME's readiness assessment.
- Review results and develop an action plan aimed at the SME's export readiness improvements.

Step 4: Export-driven Market Research

Background: XYZ is a U.S.-based SME or an external international business consulting firm. Conduct an export-related market research for XYZ

---

[18]Depending on the situational constraints and practical goals, the cost analysis, as necessary, can be expanded up to 10 criteria included in the World Bank's "Doing Business" report.

on the basis of its product line. Target market/country alternatives are limited to China, Germany, Japan, Russia, and the United States. Your analysis should result in a comparative international marketing research, strategic recommendations, and justification of XYZ's expansion to one of the aforementioned target markets/countries.

- Select a product from the SME's product line; alternatively, as part of skill development, you may select a product from business proposals/ads at http://exusa.thinkglobal.us/ (Export USA, 2017).
- On the basis of the chosen product, complete a market research resulting in the best market/country for XYZ's international export-related business expansion. Apply the step-by-step approach to market research (Step by Step Guide to Market Research, 2017) methodology (can be accessed at https://www.export.gov/article?id=Step-by-Step-Guide).[19]

References

A.M. Best Rating. 2017. Country Risks. http://www3.ambest.com/ratings/cr/crisk.aspx

Australian Trade and Investment Commission. 2017. https://www.austrade.gov.au/

Bain & Company. 2017. http://www.bain.com/publications/index.aspx

A Basic Guide to Exporting. 2016. www.export.gov/article?id=Why-Companies-should-export

Boston Consulting Group. 2017. https://www.bcg.com/

Business France. 2017. http://en.businessfrance.fr/

Carraher, S., and Welsh, D. 2017. *Global Entrepreneurship*. 3rd ed. Dubuque, IA: Kendall Hunt Publishing Company.

Coface Group. 2017. http://www.coface.com/

Competitive Alternatives. 2016. KPMG. https://www.competitivealternatives.com/

Country Commercial Guides. 2017. https://www.export.gov/ccg

Credendo. 2017. https://www.credendo.com/country_risk

Deloitte. 2017. https://www2.deloitte.com/us/en.html#

---

[19]Instead of Trade Stats Express database by the U.S. International Trade Administration (http://tse.export.gov/tse/tsehome.aspx) that is based on patterns of U.S.-centered merchandise exports and imports, users outside the United States, interested in expanding to the U.S. market should use the UN Comtrade Database (2017) at https://comtrade.un.org/ that is country neutral and integrates worldwide data.

Doing Business: Measuring Business Regulations. 2017. The World Bank. http://www.doingbusiness.org/

Ernst & Young. 2017. http://www.ey.com/us/en/industries

Export.gov portal. 2017. https://www.export.gov/services

Export Information by Industry. 2017. https://www.export.gov/industries

Export USA. 2017. http://exusa.thinkglobal.us/

Four Stages in Export Development. 2017. http://www.tradecomplianceinstitute.org/x_plfls/Four%20Stages%20of%20Export%20Development%20by%20Maurice%20Kogon.pdf

Germany: Trade and Invest. 2017. http://www.gtai.de/GTAI/Navigation/EN/welcome.html#invest

globalEDGE. 2017. https://globaledge.msu.edu/

Global Competitiveness Report 2017–2018. 2017. "World Economic Forum." http://www3.weforum.org/docs/GCR2017-2018/05FullReport/TheGlobalCompetitivenessReport2017%E2%80%932018.pdf

Gold Key Matching Service. 2017. https://build.export.gov/russia/servicesforu.s.companies/goldkeyservice/index.asp

Government of UK. Department for International Trade. 2017. https://www.gov.uk/government/organisations/department-for-international-trade.

International Energy Agency. 2017. https://www.iea.org/

International Monetary Fund. 2017. http://www.imf.org/external/index.htm

International Offices. 2017. http://2016.export.gov/worldwide_us/index.asp

International Trade Administration. 2017. http://www.trade.gov/our-services/

International Trade and Investment. 2017. Government of Canada. https://www.canada.ca/en/services/business/trade.html

International Trade Compliance Institute. 2017. http://www.tradecompliance-institute.org/

Invest in Spain. 2017. http://www.investinspain.org/invest/en/index.html

Investment Climate Statements. 2017. U.S. Department of State. https://www.state.gov/e/eb/rls/othr/ics/

Japan External Trade Organization. 2017. https://www.jetro.go.jp/en/

Korea Trade-Investment Promotion Agency. 2017. http://english.kotra.or.kr/kh/index.html

KPMG. 2017. https://home.kpmg.com/xx/en/home.html

Los Angeles Regional Export Council. 2017. http://larexc.org/

McKinsey & Company. 2017. http://www.mckinsey.com/mgi/overview

National Trade Data and Analysis. 2017. https://www.export.gov/Trade-Data-and-Analysis

Organization for Economic Cooperation and Development. 2017. http://www.oecd.org/

PricewaterhouseCoopers. 2017. https://www.pwc.com/gx/en.html

32   DOING BUSINESS IN THE UNITED STATES

Russia is Open for Your Business. 2017. http://2016.export.gov/russia/servicesforu
.s.companies/index.asp

Step by Step Guide to Market Research. 2017. https://www.export.gov/article?
id=Step-by-Step-Guide

UN Comtrade Database. 2017. https://comtrade.un.org/

UN Conference on Trade and Development. 2017. http://unctad.org/en/Pages/
Home.aspx

United Nations. 2017. http://www.un.org/en/index.html

US Commercial Service Office in Russia. 2017. http://2016.export.gov/russia/

Where We Are. 2017. https://www.export.gov/locations

World Bank. 2017. http://www.worldbank.org/?cid=ECR_GA_HPlaunch_
searchad_EN_EXTP&gclid=CJau4YP2u9QCFVBrfgodlWsMuw

World Competitiveness Yearbook. 2016. http://www.imd.org/wcc/world-
competitiveness-center-rankings/world-competitiveness-yearbook-ranking/#WCY

World Trade Organization. 2017. https://www.wto.org/

CHAPTER 2

Why the United States? Bright and Dark Sides of Doing Business in America

The greatness of America lies not in being more enlightened than any other nation, but rather in her ability to repair her faults.
—Alexis de Tocqueville (1805–1859), a French diplomat, political scientist, and historian

---

Main points in this chapter
- The United States in the global marketplace: comparative business potential and attractiveness
- Costs and risks of starting and doing business in the United States
- Small business and entrepreneurship in the United States: environment and dynamics
- Business start-up logistics in the United States

The United States in the Global Marketplace: Comparative Business Potential and Attractiveness

Strategic decisions in international business are driven by multiple, often conflicting forces, pulling (attracting) or pushing (forcing) small and medium size enterprises (SMEs) in different directions. Companies looking for expansion to overseas markets rationalize their choices by taking into consideration how these markets compare against each other in terms of their strategic benefits, business costs, and potential risks. By comparing and contrasting countries on their global marketing potential and possible threats, SMEs narrow their focus on a target country with the view of the best combination of strategic benefits, costs, and risks associated with the expansion and operation in this new market. How attractive is the U.S. marketplace relative to other countries from a foreign-based entrepreneur or SME's standpoint?

We begin by examining the United States' economic role in the world. As of 2016, the United States, the world's fourth largest geographic area, had a population of 326.6 million people, comprising 4.4 percent is too low. 5+ percent given 6+ billions world total population (third largest out of the 237 countries worldwide). It registered $18.6 trillion in GDP, purchasing power parity, comprising 15.6 percent of the world total and placing the nation third (after China and the EU) among 229 nations. United States GDP per capita, a comparative measure of economic achievement, reached $57,400 in the purchasing power parity, 20th out of 230 nations. Exports of goods and services were at $1.471 trillion or 12 percent of the world total, giving the nation a global rank of 2 (after China). Life expectancy at birth for the total population, a key measure of human/social development, was 79.8 years, 42nd of 224 worldwide (World Factbook, 2017). The United States' rank in the Yale University's environmental performance index (2017) was 26 out of 180. Its human development index was 10 out of 188 countries and territories (Human Development Report, 2017). Adding to this picture is the country's 14th out of 155 rank over 2014 to 2016 in the World Happiness Report (2017).

The World Factbook (2017) characterizes the United States as the most technologically powerful economy in the world, with U.S. firms being at or near the forefront in technological advances, especially in computers, pharmaceuticals, and medical, aerospace, and military equipment; however, their advantage has narrowed since the end of World War II. Private individuals and business firms in the United States make most of the decisions, and the federal and state governments buy needed goods and services predominantly in the private marketplace. U.S. business firms tend to enjoy greater flexibility than their counterparts in Western Europe and Japan in decisions to expand capital plant, to lay off workers, and to develop new products. At the same time, U.S.-based businesses face higher barriers to enter their rivals' home markets than foreign firms face entering U.S. markets.

Long-term problems for the United States include stagnation of wages for lower-income families, inadequate investment in deteriorating infrastructure, rapidly rising medical and pension costs of an aging population, energy shortages, and sizable current account and budget deficits. With that, depending on whether one sees the proverbial "glass half full, or half empty," these problems may be viewed as just problems. In contrast, offering and commercializing solutions to these problems may generate lucrative business opportunities.[1]

The onrush of technology has been a driving factor in the gradual development of a *two-tier* labor market in which those at the bottom lack the education and the professional/technical skills of those at the top and, more and more, fail to get comparable pay raises, health insurance coverage, and other benefits. But the globalization of trade, and especially the rise of low-wage producers such as China, has put additional downward pressure on wages and upward pressure on the return to capital. Since 1975, practically all the gains in household income have gone to the top 20 percent of households. Since 1996, dividends and capital gains have grown faster than wages or any other category of after-tax income.

Imported oil accounts for nearly 55 percent of U.S. consumption and, with this staggering share, oil has a major impact on the overall health of the American economy. Crude oil prices doubled between 2001 and 2006, the year home prices peaked; higher gasoline prices ate into consumers' budgets and many individuals fell behind in their mortgage payments. Oil prices climbed another 50 percent between 2006 and 2008, and bank foreclosures more than doubled in the same period. Besides dampening the housing market, soaring oil prices caused a drop in the

---

[1]Numerous business periodical publications discuss entrepreneurial business venture ideas, start-ups, and success stories. For example, *Entrepreneur* profiles the latest trends and insights on business opportunities (https://www.entrepreneur.com/bizopportunities); *Forbes* publishes the annual list of 25 young U.S. companies with a strong chance at reaching a valuation of $1 billion or more (https://www.forbes.com/sites/susanadams/2017/09/26/the-next-billion-dollar-startups-2017/#3d8ba6ba4447); *Fortune* publishes useful articles under the Entrepreneurship rubric (http://fortune.com/tag/entrepreneurship/). *Bloomberg Businessweek,* the *Wall Street Journal,* and many other U.S.-based publications also publish stories offering advice, analysis, and inspiration on entrepreneurship and start-ups in the United States.

value of the dollar and a deterioration in the U.S. merchandise trade deficit, which peaked at $840 billion in 2008. Because the U.S. economy is energy-intensive, falling oil prices since 2013 have alleviated many of the problems the earlier increases had created (World Factbook, 2017).

Gross national saving rates in the United States tend to be low compared with other countries, suggesting a tendency to spend rather than save—good news to the marketers. In 2016, U.S. savings stood at 18.6 percent of GDP, placing the country 105th out of 181 countries worldwide and below the 28.6 percent world average. Table 2.1 contrasts U.S. current macroeconomic structure with that of China, Germany, and Japan.[2] Table 2.1 reveals the Unites States' comparatively larger share of private household consumption, lower share of investment in fixed capital, and smaller role of exports/imports in the national economy. Additionally, while services generate a dominant share of economic output, industry plays a lesser role in the national GDP.

According to Euromonitor International (aka Passport), a leading international marketing consultancy, American *agriculture* accounts for a small portion of GDP and employs just 1.6 percent of the workforce; farming is predominately large scale and generally efficient and competitive. The United States is among the world's major exporters of foodstuffs and processed foods. Increased productivity is the main driver of agricultural growth. The *manufacturing* sector contributes 12.4 percent of GDP and employs 10.4 percent of the workforce. Leading industries include aerospace, telecommunications, chemicals, electronics and computers. *Services* account for 79.2 percent of GDP. The most important activities in the service sector include real estate, transport, finance, healthcare, and business services. In the financial sector, lending standards are being tightened. The real value of tourist receipts rose by 0.5 percent in 2016 and growth of 3 percent was projected for 2017. The slowdown in tourist receipts is partially due to the rise in the value of the U.S. dollar against other currencies. Retail sales were expected to rise in 2017 but consumers'

---

[2]Germany and Japan are included for contrast as comparators as world's largest powers from the category of innovation driven economies. China illustrates patterns of a major global power categorized in the Global Competitiveness Report (2017) at Stage 2: Efficiency-driven (30 economies).

Table 2.1 The United States, China, Germany, and Japan: selected comparative macroeconomic indicators, % of GDP, 2016 (est.)

	United States	China*	Germany	Japan
Savings rate, %	18.6	46.0	27.9	25.3
GDP composition by end use				
Household consumption	68.6	37.1	53.7	58.3
Government consumption	17.7	14.0	19.5	20.4
Investment in fixed capital	15.9	43.7	20.1	21.7
Investment in inventories	0.5	1.6	−1.0	−0.1
Exports of goods and services	12.0	22.0	45.7	16.6
Imports of goods and services	−14.7	18.5	−38.0	−6.9
GDP composition by sector of origin				
Agriculture	1.1	8.6	0.6	1.2
Industry	19.4	39.8	30.3	27.7
Services	79.5	51.6	69.1	71.1

*2015 (est.)
Source: World Factbook. 2017. https://www.cia.gov/library/publications/the-world-factbook/

shift away from brick-and-mortar shopping is hurting many big retailers (U.S. Country Profile, 2017).

The United States' attractiveness as a marketplace relative to other countries can be assessed by looking at two dozen global indexes (rankings) on the United States' country page at globalEDGE (2017). For example, some global indexes reveal that U.S. corruption perception index is 18/176; DHL global connectedness index, 27/140; ease of doing business rank, 8/190; global manufacturing competitiveness index, 2/40; and international logistics performance index, 10/160. In rationalizing a country selection decision, a company contemplating international expansion to the United States can compile and prioritize a list of global indexes and take the country's standing on those dimensions into consideration in its expansion decision.

Further steps in analyzing the United States' national business landscape may involve Trading Economics (2017): This statistical portal contains more than 200 macro indicators characterizing the United States' socioeconomic profile and developments nationwide as well as selected economic sectors and areas. Even a simple cross-country analysis on the basis of 11 parameters in Trading Economics provides a visual picture of the country's comparative attractiveness from a macroeconomic perspective. Examining some of the macroeconomic indicators of critical importance and relevance to a specific industry under consideration in a more detailed comparative format (the United States versus alternative country comparator) may also be a useful part of the background research.

In addition, indicators of global competitiveness can serve as a critical measure of the nation's attractiveness in international business: National rankings and profiles in the global competitiveness surveys are essentially determined by the factors similar to those making this nation an attractive marketplace. Situationally, these factors may range from strengths of its political–economic institutions to quality of the infrastructure, to innovations. In this context, the latest annual Global Competitiveness Report (GCR 2017) positions the United States as the world's second most competitive nation out of 137 countries included in the survey. Figure 2.1 represents the United States' global competiveness and by extension—business attractiveness—in comparison with the European and North American regions over the past few years. As the chart shows, in the latest 2016 survey, the United States demonstrates superior competiveness against both the European and the North American regions on most of the parameters except for the macroeconomic environment category where the U.S. position is weaker.

Another authoritative source of information and analytical tool in cross-country global competitiveness is the annual World Competitiveness Yearbook (WCY). The latest 2017 survey places the United States' global competitiveness at 4, following Hong Kong SAR, Switzerland, and Singapore (World Competitiveness Yearbook, 2017).

Going international places the company in an external political–economic environment that may be very different from that of its home

Index Component	Rank/137	Score (1-7)	Trend	Distance from best	Edition	2012-13	2013-14	2014-15	2015-16	2016-17	2017-18
Global Competitiveness Index	2	5.9	—		Rank	7 / 144	5 / 148	3 / 144	3 / 140	3 / 138	2 / 137
Subindex A: Basic requirements	25	5.5			Score	5.5	5.5	5.5	5.6	5.7	5.9
1st pillar: Institutions	20	5.3									
2nd pillar: Infrastructure	9	6.0									
3rd pillar: Macroeconomic environment	83	4.5									
4th pillar: Health and primary education	29	6.3									
Subindex B: Efficiency enhancers	1	6.0									
5th pillar: Higher education and training	3	6.1									
6th pillar: Goods market efficiency	7	5.5									
7th pillar: Labor market efficiency	3	5.6									
8th pillar: Financial market development	2	5.7									
9th pillar: Technological readiness	6	6.2									
10th pillar: Market size	2	6.9									
Subindex C: Innovation and sophistication factors	2	5.8									
11th pillar: Business sophistication	2	5.8									
12th pillar: Innovation	2	5.8									

■ United States   Europe and North America

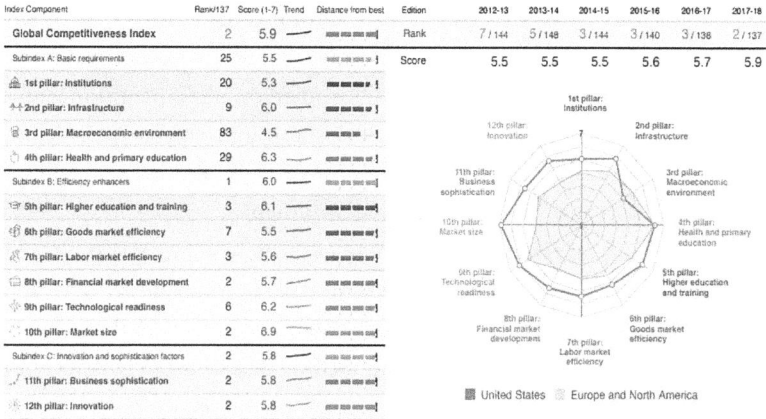

Figure 2.1 The United States vs. Europe and North America: performance in global competitiveness

Source: Global Competitiveness Report 2017–2018. 2017. http://www3.weforum.org/docs/GCR2017-2018/05FullReport/TheGlobalCompetitivenessReport2017%E2%80%932018.pdf

country. In a broad strategic sense, the business environment can be defined as a set of interdependent factors or variables that together comprise the political, economic, social, technological, legal, and environmental (PESTLE) framework.[3] PESTLE parameters and their importance vary across countries and have an impact on the country's attractiveness in the company's comparative strategic perspective in relation to the company's situation context. Different mixtures of these variables across countries translate into different business outcomes, including effectiveness (maximizing results), efficiency (minimizing costs), and risks (that can be optimized/mitigated in a strategic decision). Although, unlike big corporations, SMEs have limited power in influencing the business environment in a host country due to their small size, they still should be aware of PESTLE's state, trends, and dynamics in order to stay viable and competitive.

---

[3]A PESTLE analysis looks at a framework of macro factors used in the business environmental scanning aspect of strategic management. Sometimes instead of PESTLE, a narrower PEST format is used in the same analytical context by excluding from separate consideration legal and environmental components.

- PESTLE Analysis *Political* may examine the impacts of government type and dynamics; democracy, freedom of press, rule of law, law enforcement, and levels of bureaucracy and corruption; trends in deregulation and privatization; social and employment legislation; tax policy and trade and tariff controls; and trends and likely developments in the political environment.
- PESTLE Analysis *Economic* may examine the impacts of stage of business cycle, current state and projected economic growth, inflation and interest rates, unemployment and labor supply and costs, levels of disposable income and income distribution, globalization, likely technological or other change on the economy, and likely changes in the economic environment.
- PESTLE Analysis *Social* may examine the impacts of demographics (population growth rate and age composition); population health, education and social mobility, and attitudes toward these; population employment patterns; job market freedom and attitudes toward work; press attitudes, public opinion, social attitudes and taboos; lifestyle choices and attitudes toward these; sociocultural trends and changes; and health consciousness.
- PESTLE Analysis *Technology* may examine the impacts of emerging technologies; the Internet, reduction in communication costs, and increased remote working; R&D activity; technology transfer; degree of automation; and rate of technological change.
- PESTLE Analysis *Legal* may examine the impacts of antitrust law, consumer law, discrimination law, employment law, and health and safety laws.
- PESTLE Analysis *Environmental* may examine the impacts of weather, natural disasters, climate, climate change, environmental taxes, and demand for *green* products (University of Central Florida Libraries 2017).

More specifically, the selection and prioritization of the United States' PESTLE parameters in an SME's strategy depends on its background, current business position, future aspirations, strengths and weaknesses, industry it operates in, market drivers and constraints specific to this industry and markets, and other conditions.

In addition to awareness of the general characteristics of the market-place, an SME doing business in the United States needs to take into account the state, trends, dynamics, competitive environment, and out-look specific to the industry in which it operates.

In general, industry analysis involves assessment of:

- *industry size* (output, supply, demand), industry leaders, their out-put shares, and strategic positions in the market;
- *industry structure* (concentrated versus fragmented);
- developmental *drivers* and *constraints* and *patterns* and *trends* in performance and output over a period of time (upward, down-ward, or stagnant; stable or erratic; cyclical or random);
- *growth rates* and *patterns* over a period of time.
- *future trends, development,* and *opportunities* (products, technolo-gies, processes, markets);
- *economic dynamics* (profitability, return on investment);
- *cost structure* (main cost factors, dynamics over a period of time);
- *marketing mix* (the 4Ps—products, pricing, place/distribution, promotion—and their trends and dynamics);
- *critical success factors* (innovation, cost efficiency, global outreach);
- *social, environmental, sustainable performance* (external environ-mental factors: regulations, policies and politics, social responsi-bility norms; internal environmental factors: prevalent corporate internal attitudes toward employees, customer, and shareholders);
- *competitive analysis* (industry's competitive environment along the SWOT, Porter's 5-force competitive framework, or 4Ps marketing mix framework (global, geo-regional, national, or regional levels).

There are numerous public and commercial databases containing industry and market reports specific to the United States. Some examples of the databases in public access are globalEDGE/countries/United States (2017), Los Angeles Economic Development Corporation (2017), and Export Development Canada (2017). Some examples of the commercial databases are IBIS World (2017), Euromonitor International (2017), and Business Source Complete (2017). Access to commercial databases tends to be expensive, but many of them can be accessed by qualified users complimentary at universities of higher education and major national public libraries in the United States.

A country as large and diverse as the United States is characterized by remarkable political–economic, demographic, and cultural variations across states, regions, and municipalities. The importance of this regional analytical dimension is compelled by cross-state and cross-regional dissimilarities that result in different comparative business pros/cons, costs, and risks. There is a vast array of rankings, analytical frameworks, databases, and sources of regional information and assistance in the United States ranging from government agencies to private sources to nonprofit organizations and universities. In the interest of space and time, we will just mention three public sources of analytical information that can be useful for a comparative assessment of business environment and attractiveness at the state and municipal level.

U.S. News & World Report (2017) publishes its annual "Best States Rankings" report that measures outcomes and attractiveness for citizens on the basis of more than 60 metrics. The report ranks the 50 states of the United States on the basis of the following criteria important for business in various ways: overall, state health care, education, crime & corrections, infrastructure, opportunity, economy, and government. Table 2.2. provides an example illustrating California's rankings. In addition to numerical rankings across seven criteria, the Best States Rankings database offers access to extensive statistics comparing California and the 49 other states with "comparator states" on multiple parameters.

The globalEDGE (2017) database provides another analytical alternative and access to state information in the business context. Under the rubric "Global Insights," section "By State," there is an information designated

Table 2.2 California's ranking among the 50 states of the United States (1 is the best, 50 is the worst)

Overall rank	Health care	Education	Crime and corrections	Infrastructure	Opportunity	Economy	Government
23	10	25	20	33	42	3	44

Source: U.S. News & World Report. 2017. "Best States Rankings." https://www.usnews.com/news/best-states/rankings

for international business and trade on the 50 states in the United States. In addition to demographic, economic, and historical information on each state, the database hosts data on corporations with headquarters in the state and links to state-specific resources.[4] The section "Resources" opens access to additional sources of analytical and factual information from state government agencies and nonprofit organizations. Figure 2.2 provides a screenshot of the State of California's home page in the globalEDGE database.

SizeUp, a business analytical portal hosted on the U.S. Small Business Administration (SBA) site, is yet another useful tool. As a major federal agency charged with facilitation and support of small business and entrepreneurship nationwide, SBA provides a range of services that includes free information support and business counseling. SBA's database contains "Business Guide" that offers extensive resources on planning, launching, managing, and growing small business. These resources include the SizeUp analytical tool.[5] SizeUp allows small business owners and entrepreneurs to compare how their business stacks up with the competition in order to succeed. SizeUp helps managing and growing business by benchmarking it against competitors; mapping customers, competitors, and suppliers; and locating the best places to advertise (U.S. Small Business Administration, 2017). Figure 2.3. exemplifies the

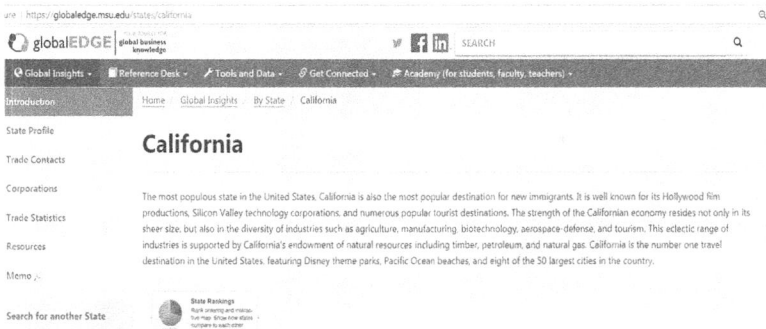

Figure 2.2 State of California in globalEDGE

Source: globalEDGE. 2017. https://globaledge.msu.edu/

---

[4]The site also provides states' rankings on 20 socio-economic parameters making it an effective analytical tool in cross-state comparisons.

[5]It can also be accessed directly at SizeUp (2017).

SizeUp analytical framework. After completing a free registration, the user is asked to enter the following nine parameters in the section "My Business": annual revenue, year the business was started, average annual worker salary, number of full-time employees, cost effectiveness, revenue generated per community resident, local turnover (percentage of workers newly hired), health care costs per employee, and workers' compensation premium per employee. A local map generated in the section "Competition" shows competitors, customers, and suppliers specific to the local geographic area and the industry. The section "Advertising" generates another map, which marks the best places to advertise that are specific to the local geographic area and the industry on the basis of the indicator of total revenue. In the latter case, the SizeUp tool provides several links, each leading to a market profile for a respective location specific to the inquiry.

Figures 2.4 and 2.5 represent an example of a market profile for West Carson, a town in Greater Los Angeles, on the SizeUp analytical radar. By critically examining this profile and putting it in a comparative market perspective against other alternative regions or municipalities, an SME or individual entrepreneur can better rationalize a decision in regional strategic targeting within the United States.

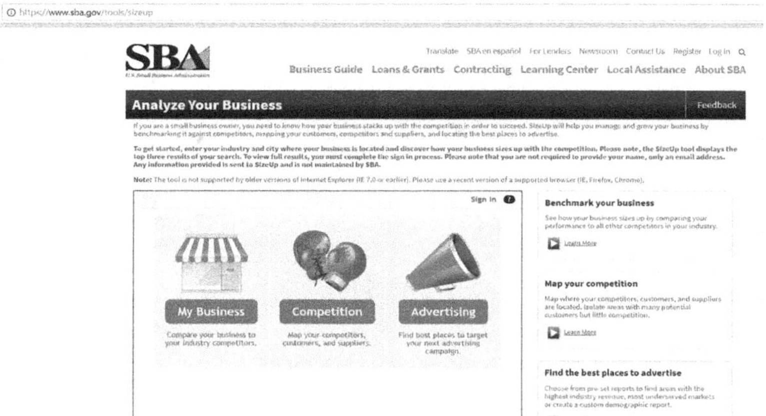

Figure 2.3 SizeUp analytical tool

Source: U.S. Small Business Administration. Office of Advocacy. 2017. https://www.sba.gov/sites/default/files/advocacy/SB-FAQ-2016_WEB.pdf.

https://www.sizeup.com/community/california/los-angeles/west-carson-cdp

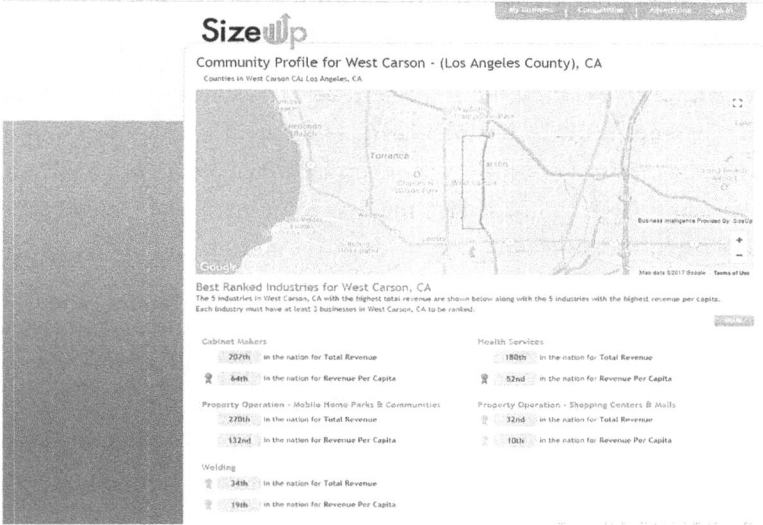

Figure 2.4 Community profile for West Carson (a)

Source: SizeUp. 2017. https://www.sizeup.com/

View a complete list of industries in West Carson, CA

Community Demographics for West Carson, CA

People		Labor Force Quality	
Population:	21,810	Bachelors Degree or Higher:	32.6%
Labor Force:	11,115	Highschool Degree or Higher:	84.9%
Small Businesses:	993	White Collar Workers:	65.6%
Job Growth (2000-2010):	4.9%	Blue Collar Workers:	34.2%
Unemployment Rate:	N/A	Very Creative Professionals:	N/A
Median Age:	41.25	Creative Professionals:	N/A
		Young and Educated:	5.0%
Budgets		International Talent:	0.1%
Household Expenditures (Average):	$62,143	Universities in Community:	2
Household Income:	$63,885	Universities in Community + 50 miles:	106
Top State Personal Income Tax:	N/A	Commute Time:	26 minutes
Top State Personal Capital Gains Tax:	N/A		
Top State Corporate Income Tax:	N/A		
Top State Corporate Capital Gains Tax:	N/A		
State Sales Tax:	N/A		
Property Tax:	0.6%		
Home Value:	$444,100		

Figure 2.5 Community profile for West Carson (Los Angeles County) CA (b)

Source: SizeUp. 2017. https://www.sizeup.com/

Costs and Risks of Starting and Doing Business in the United States

Earlier, we emphasized the strategic triad in business decision making that includes benefits, business costs, and potential risks. By comparing and contrasting countries on their global market appeal, SMEs can select their target country with the best combination of strategic benefits, costs, and risks associated with the expansion and operation in a new market.

With the United States' reputation as the world's prime and potentially attractive market for many industrial products and consumer goods and services, for expanding to and doing business in the United States the second item of the triad—costs—should be taken into consideration. These costs vary across economic sectors and industries. One of the best public sources of comparative information on the ease and cost of doing business at the national level is the annual "Doing Business"

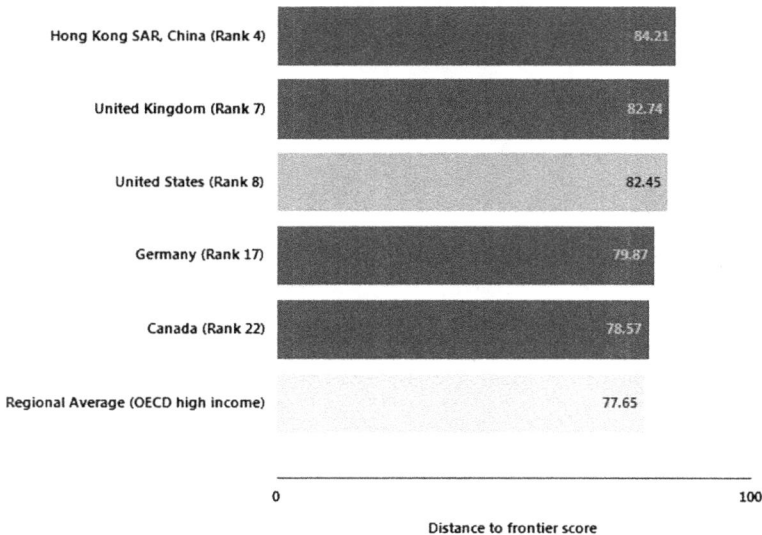

Hong Kong SAR, China (Rank 4)	84.21
United Kingdom (Rank 7)	82.74
United States (Rank 8)	82.45
Germany (Rank 17)	79.87
Canada (Rank 22)	78.57
Regional Average (OECD high income)	77.65

0   100

Distance to frontier score

Figure 2.6 How the United States and comparator economies rank on the ease of doing business

Source: Doing Business 2017. Economy Profile 2017. United States. World Bank Group. http://www.doingbusiness.org/~/media/wbg/doingbusiness/documents/profiles/country/usa.pdf and United States (2017).

Starting a Business (51)

Resolving Insolvency (5)   Dealing with Construction Permits (39)

Enforcing Contracts (20)   Getting Electricity (36)

Trading across Borders (35)   Registering Property (36)

Paying Taxes (36)   Getting Credit (2)

Protecting Minority Investors (41)

Figure 2.7 Rankings on "Doing Business" topics—United States: ease/cost of doing business

Source: Doing Business 2017. Economy Profile 2017. United States. World Bank Group. http://www.doingbusiness.org/~/media/wbg/doingbusiness/documents/profiles/country/usa.pdf and United States (2017).

Starting a Business (91.23)

Resolving Insolvency (89.19)   Dealing with Construction Permits (75.74)

Enforcing Contracts (72.61)   Getting Electricity (83.39)

Trading across Borders (92.01)   Registering Property (76.80)

Paying Taxes (83.85)   Getting Credit (95.00)

Protecting Minority Investors (64.67)

Figure 2.8 Number of small businesses in the United States

Source: U.S. Small Business Administration: Office of Advocacy. 2016. Small Business Profile. https://www.sba.gov/sites/default/files/advocacy/United_States.pdf

survey (World Bank 2017). The latest "Doing Business" report[6] ranks the United States eighth in the world. Figures 2.6 through 2.8 and Table 2.3 depict America's comparative profile in this latest survey.

_____

[6]The Doing Business 2017 is the 14th in a series of World Bank's annual reports investigating regulations that enhance business activity and those that constrain it. The report provides quantitative indicators in 190 economies covering 11 areas of the business environment: Starting a business, Dealing with construction permits, Getting electricity, Registering property, Getting credit, Protecting minority investors, Paying taxes, Trading across borders, Enforcing contracts, Resolving insolvency, and Labor market regulation (World Bank, 2017). In addition to global rankings, Doing Business contains specific information on the ease/cost of doing business within each of these categories for each country.

Table 2.3 *Selected indicators of the ease/cost of doing business: the United States vs. comparator countries*

Indicator	United States DB2017	United States DB2016	New York City DB2017	Los Angeles DB2017	Germany DB2017	UK DB2017	Best performer globally DB2017
Starting a business							
World rank (out of 190 economies)	51	45	–	–	114	16	1 (New Zealand)
Time—men (days)	5.6	5.6	4.0	8.0	10.5	4.5	0.5 (New Zealand)
Cost—men (% of income per capita)	1.1	1.1	1.3	0.8	1.9	0.1	0.0 (Slovenia)
Time—women (days)	5.6	5.6	4.0	8.0	10.5	4.5	0.5 (New Zealand)
Cost—women (% of income per capita)	1.1	1.1	1.3	0.8	1.9	0.1	0.0 (Slovenia)
Dealing with construction permits							
World rank	39	37	–	–	12	17	1 (New Zealand)
DTF score	75.74	75.73	73.43	79.21	81.45	80.34	87.40 (New Zealand)
Time (days)	80.6	80.6	89.0	68.0	96.0	86.0	28.0 (Korea, Rep.)
Cost (% of warehouse value)	1.0	1.0	0.3	1.9	1.1	1.1	0.1 (Trinidad and Tobago)

Getting electricity							
World rank (out of 190)	36	32	–	–	5	17	1 (Korea, Rep.)
Time (days)	89.6	89.6	60.0	134.0	28.0	79.0	18.0 (Korea, Rep.*)
Cost (% of income per capita)	24.4	24.6	14.0	40.0	40.8	25.8	0.0 (Japan)
Registering property							
World rank	36	37	–	–	79	47	1 (New Zealand)
DTF score	76.80	76.85	76.66	77.02	65.72	74.11	94.46 (New Zealand)
Time (days)	15.2	15.2	12.0	20.0	52.00	21.5	1.0 (Economies*)
Cost (% of property value)	2.4	2.4	3.5	0.9	6.7	4.8	0.0 (Saudi Arabia)
Getting credit							
World rank	2	2	–	–	32	20	1 (New Zealand)
Getting credit (DTF Score)	95.00	95.00	95.00	95.00	70.00	75.00	100 (New Zealand)
Protecting minority investors							
Rank	41	39	–	–	53	6	1 (New Zealand)
DTF score	64.67	64.67	63.33	66.67	60.00	78.33	88.33 (New Zealand)

(Continued)

Table 2.3 Selected indicators of the ease/cost of doing business: the United States vs. comparator countries (Continued)

Indicator	United States DB2017	United States DB2016	New York City DB2017	Los Angeles DB2017	Germany DB2017	UK DB2017	Best performer globally DB2017
Paying taxes							
World rank	36	34	–	–	48	10	1 (United Emirates)
DTF score	83.85	83.89	82.92	85.25	82.10	90.74	99.44 (United Emirates)
Time (hours per year)	175.0	175.0	175.0	175.0	218.00	110.0	55.0 (Luxembourg)
Total tax rate (% of profit)	44.0	43.9	46.0	40.9	48.9	30.9	26.1 (32 Economies*)
Trading across borders							
World rank	35	35	–	–	38	28	1 (10 Economies*)
DTF score	92.01	92.01	92.01	92.01	91.77	93.76	100.00 (10 Economies*)
Cost to export: Border compliance (USD)	175	175	175	175	345	280	0 (18 Economies*)
Cost to export: Documentary compliance (USD)	60	60	60	60	45	25	0 (19 Economies*)
Cost to import: Border compliance (USD)	175	175	175	175	0	0	0 (28 Economies*)

50

Cost to import: Documentary compliance (USD)	100	100	100	100	0	0	0 (30 Economies*)

Enforcing contracts

World rank	20	20	–	17	31		1 (Korea, Rep.)
DTF Score	72.61	72.61	79.06	62.93	73.17	69.36	84.15 (Korea, Rep.)
Time (days)	420.0	420.0	370.0	495.0	499.0	437.0	164.0 (Singapore)
Cost (% of claim)	30.5	30.5	22.9	42.0	14.4	43.9	9.0 (Iceland)

Resolving insolvency

World rank	5	4	–	3	13		1 (Finland)
DTF score	89.19	89.20	89.19	89.19	92.28	82.04	93.89 (Finland)
Recovery rate (cents on the dollar)	78.6	78.6	78.6	78.6	84.4	88.6	92.9 (Norway)
Time (years)	1.5	1.5	1.5	1.5	1.2	1.0	0.4 (22 Economies*)
Cost (% of estate)	10.0	10.0	10.0	10.0	8.0	6.0	1.0 (22 Economies*)

*Two or more economies share the top ranking on this indicator. A number shown in place of an economy's name indicates the number of economies that share the top ranking on the indicator. For a list of these economies, see the "Doing Business" website (www.doingbusiness.org).

Source: Doing Business 2017. 2017. Economy Profile 2017. United States. World Bank Group. http://www.doingbusiness.org/~/media/wbg/doingbusiness/documents/profiles/country/usa.pdf

Source: Doing Business. Measuring Business Regulations (2017).

The cost of doing business in the nation varies across regions/municipalities and industries.[7] Therefore, it is imperative to engage regional—particularly state-specific—sources for a more detailed cost analysis. For example, in the case of California it may be beneficial to begin by examining the California Government (2017) site and, depending on the specific situation, interest, or issue, continue analysis by tapping selected California government agencies (the list of agencies on the California Government site includes 157 entries).

The California Governor's Office of Business and Economic Development (GO-Biz, 2017) offers a range of specific services tailored toward business owners. These services include attraction, retention, and expansion services; site selection; permit assistance; regulatory guidance; small business assistance; international trade development; assistance with state government; and much more. Companies and entrepreneurs interested in starting and growing a business can find information and government assistance on starting a business, relocating or expanding a business, international trade and investment, financial assistance, closing a business, and emergency preparedness and recovery (GO-Biz, 2017).

Within the state of California, the largest in the nation, many counties, cities, and rural municipalities have their own government agencies, information resources, and business development and government assistance programs. Examples of these regional units include the County of Los Angeles (2017), the Los Angeles Economic Development Corporation (2017), and the city of Carson (2017). Numerous think tanks (Milken Family Foundation, 2017), nonprofit organizations (California Center for Jobs and the Economy, 2017; World Trade Center Los Angeles, 2017), academic institutions such as the Institute for Strategy & Competitiveness at Harvard Business School (Porter, 2012), business consultancies

---

[7]Industry cost structure is determined by factors of production. Depending on these factors, industries may be labor intensive, capital intensive, require significant amount of land, involve high level of education, skills, be economically driven by burden of regulatory compliance, litigations, or environmental compliance. For example, the biennial "Competitive Alternatives" survey by KPMG, a global business consultancy, provides information on business costs and compares these costs across 19 industries in more than 100 cities in 10 countries worldwide, including the United States (Competitive Alternatives, 2016).

(McKinsey, 2017), private sector sources, and periodical publications can be also engaged, depending on the scope, depth, time, and other situational parameters and constraints involved in a specific business research. As in the California example, this approach with necessary modifications can be applied to conducting business research in other states across the United States.

Small Business and Entrepreneurship in the United States: Environment and Dynamics

Small business and entrepreneurship[8] is a foundation of the U.S. economy and historically has played a vital political–economic and societal role. The SBA defines *small business* in general as an independent business having fewer than 500 employees.[9] In the following paragraphs we summarize major facts about the U.S. small business sector that may be of interest to individual entrepreneurs and SMEs aspiring to start and grow business in the country.

---

[8]The term *entrepreneur* is often used in a similar context or even interchangeably with the term *small business*. While most entrepreneurial ventures are originally born as a small business, not all small businesses are entrepreneurial. Many small businesses in the United States are sole proprietorships consisting just of the owner, or they have a small number of employees; many of these small businesses offer an existing product, process, or service, and they do not aim at growth. These small businesses are sometimes categorized as lifestyle ventures. In contrast, genuine entrepreneurial ventures tend to offer an innovative product, process, or service, pursue a competitive business model, and the entrepreneur typically aims to scale up the company by adding employees, seeking international sales, and so on, a process that is financed by banks, venture capital, angel investments, or even government sources. Successful entrepreneurs have the ability to lead a business in a positive direction by proper planning, to adapt to changing environments, and to understand their own strengths and weakness (Driessen and Zwart, 2010). Being driven by competitive market forces and their own motivations often funded by outside sources, entrepreneurs tend to be more prone to risk taking and a pursuit of aggressive growth of their business ventures compared with small business owners. For additional details please refer to Shobhit (2017).
[9]Industry-specific definitions of small business used in U.S. government programs and contracting vary (for details see www.sba.gov/content/small-business-size-standards).

As of 2014, there were 29.6 million registered small businesses in the United States. Eighty percent, or 23.8 million, of these businesses had no employees (they are termed *nonemployers*); 20 percent, or 5.8 million, had paid employees. The number of small business employers has increased after a decline during the recession and the number of nonemployers has gradually increased, from 15.4 million in 1997 to 23.8 million in 2014 (Figure 2.9).

Distribution of small firms by industry in the United States is presented in Figure 2.10. As this chart reveals, professional, scientific, and technical services; construction; and health care and social assistance industries tend to have the highest representation of small firms across all four categories: firms with 1–499 employees, 1–19 employees, nonemployer firms, and the total number of small firms. The real estate and rental and leasing industry also demonstrates a high presence of small firms in the nonemployer category and total count.

Small businesses constitute 99.9 percent of all registered firms in the United States, 99.7 percent of firms with paid employees, 97.6 percent of exporting firms (287,835 small exporters), 32.9 percent of known export value ($440 billion out of $1.3 trillion), 47.8 percent of private sector employees (58 million out of 121 million employees), and 41.1 percent

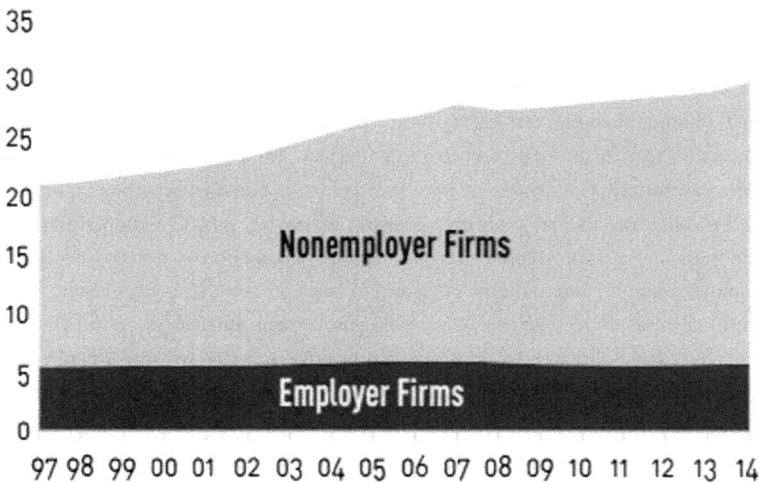

Figure 2.9 Distance to frontier scores on "Doing Business" topics— The United States' distance to frontier scores on the cost/ease of doing business

Source: Small Business Profile, 2016.

Industry	1 – 499 Employees	1 – 19 Employees	Nonemployer Firms	Total Small Firms
Professional, Scientific, and Technical Services	778,090	731,341	3,235,906	4,013,996
Other Services (except Public Administration)	670,468	626,850	3,583,742	4,254,210
Retail Trade	649,764	595,280	1,906,597	2,556,361
Construction	645,479	598,039	2,368,442	3,013,921
Health Care and Social Assistance	642,586	561,706	1,959,723	2,602,309
Accommodation and Food Services	502,076	397,330	346,280	848,356
Administrative, Support, and Waste Management	325,474	289,799	2,032,516	2,357,990
Wholesale Trade	309,568	267,370	406,469	716,037
Real Estate and Rental and Leasing	275,298	262,850	2,448,282	2,723,580
Manufacturing	248,155	188,964	343,025	591,180
Finance and Insurance	233,184	216,130	706,394	939,578
Transportation and Warehousing	167,496	149,262	1,102,255	1,269,751
Arts, Entertainment, and Recreation	116,159	100,867	1,256,694	1,372,853
Educational Services	85,151	67,144	616,952	702,103
Information	70,792	61,051	326,526	397,318
Mining, Quarrying, and Oil and Gas Extraction	21,594	18,222	106,610	128,204
Agriculture, Forestry, Fishing and Hunting	21,323	19,997	239,863	261,186
Utilities	5,715	4,511	19,344	25,059
Total	**5,768,372**	**5,156,713**	**23,005,620**	**28,773,992**

Totals for Tables 1 and 2 differ from SUSB's nationwide tallies due to firms with establishments in more than one industry and the omission of industry classifications not reported by NES. (Source: NES and SUSB)
s Indicates samples deemed too small to represent the population according to SUSB.

Figure 2.10 U.S. small firms by industry

Source: U.S. Small Business Administration. Office of Advocacy. 2017. https://www.sba.gov/sites/default/files/advocacy/SB-FAQ-2016_WEB.pdf.

of private sector payroll. Out of all new business establishments started in 2015, 79.9 percent survived until 2016, the highest share since 2006. From 2005 to 2015, an average of 78.5 percent of new establishments survived 1 year. About half of all establishments survived 5 years or longer. In the past decade, this ranged from a low of 45.4 percent for establishments started in 2006, and a high of 51 percent for those started in 2011. About one-third of establishments survive 10 years or longer. Some data sources suggest that about two out of three establishment exits are the result of firm closures (Small Business Data Resources, 2017; U.S. Small Business Administration: Office of Advocacy, 2016).

The small business start-up rates only slightly exceed the closure rates: In 2014, there were about 404,000 start-ups (firms less than one year old) and 392,000 firm closures. As illustrated in Figure 2.11, market forces and dynamics create a very competitive environment for small business and entrepreneurship in the United States, where, to use the Darwinian phrase, only the fittest can survive and succeed. Put simply,

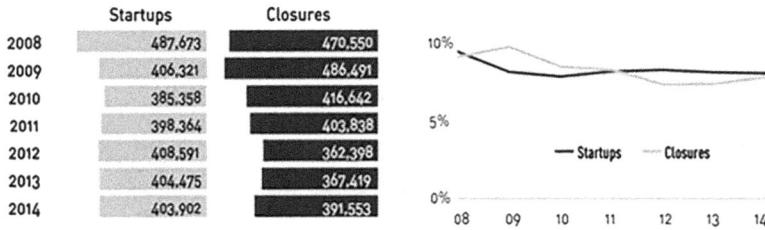

	Startups	Closures
2008	487,673	470,550
2009	406,321	486,491
2010	385,358	416,642
2011	398,364	403,838
2012	408,591	362,398
2013	404,475	367,419
2014	403,902	391,553

Figure 2.11 Employer firm start-ups and closures in the United States

Source: U.S. Small Business Administration: Office of Advocacy. 2016. Small Business Profile. https://www.sba.gov/sites/default/files/advocacy/United_States.pdf

everybody here has the freedom to pursue an entrepreneurial dream, but the flip side of this is a similar freedom to fail.

Indicatively, about one-seventh, or 14.4 percent, of business owners in the United States are immigrants. The industries with the greatest share of immigrant owners tend to be accommodation and food services (29.1 percent of owners were foreign born) and transportation and warehousing (27.5 percent). About one in five firms (19.3 percent) is family owned. Of these family-owned firms, about half are *equally owned*, that is, 50 percent owned by one or more men and 50 percent owned by one or more women. Hence, about one in 10 firms is both family owned and equally owned. The industries with the highest share of family-owned firms are management of companies and enterprises (46.4 percent of firms in this industry are family owned), real estate and rental and leasing (37.3 percent), and accommodation and food services (33.2 percent). The industries with the highest share of equally owned firms are real estate and rental and leasing (18.6 percent of firms in this industry are equally owned); mining, quarrying, and oil and gas extraction (16.9 percent); and accommodation and food services (16.9 percent). A home-based business is operated primarily out of one's home, but business activities may take place at other locations as well. The share of businesses that are home based has remained relatively constant over the past decade, at about 50 percent of all firms. More specifically, 60.1 percent of all firms without paid employees are home based, as are 23.3 percent of small employer firms and 0.3 percent of large employer firms. The industries in which businesses are most likely to be home based are information (70 percent), construction (68.2 percent), and professional, scientific, and technical services

(65.3 percent). Meanwhile, 2.3 percent of nonemployer firms, 5.3 percent of small employers, and 9.6 percent of large employers are franchises.

The economic size of start-ups has fluctuated over the past decade, but in 2014 an average employment reached a four-year high of 6.1 employees. Average employment at firms of all ages has increased slightly during this period, from 22.4 employees per firm in 2005 to 23.5 employees per firm in 2014. The most common source of capital to finance business expansion is personal and family savings (21.9 percent of small firms), followed by business profits and assets (5.7 percent), business loans from financial institutions (4.5 percent), and business credit cards from banks (3.3 percent). In fiscal year (FY) 2016, 24.3 percent of contracting dollars went to small businesses, down from 25.8 percent in FY 2015 and 25.1 percent in FY 2014. Of agencies with at least $1 billion in eligible contract dollars, the ones that awarded the highest share of contracting dollars to small businesses were the U.S. Departments of the Interior (59.8 percent), Agriculture (56.3 percent), and Transportation (52.0 percent) (Small Business Dashboard 2017; Small Business Data Resources 2017).

In 2014, there were 248,122 small employer firms in high-tech industries, representing 98.5 percent of all employer firms in these industries. The majority of these small firms provide services in either computer systems design or architecture and engineering (Figure 2.12). Among small firms, the industries with the highest growth from 2012 to 2014 were software publishers and computer systems design services (Figure 2.13).

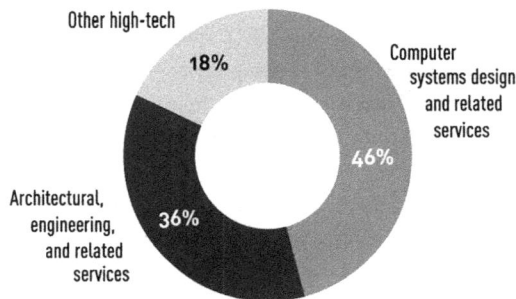

Figure 2.12 Small firms in high-tech industries in the United States, 2014

Source: U.S. Small Business Administration: Office of Advocacy. 2017. https://www.sba.gov/sites/default/files/advocacy/SB-FAQ-2016_WEB.pdf.

NAICS code	Industry name	Small firms	Large firms
5112	Software publishers	9.8	12.6
5415	Computer systems design	3.3	1.4
3254	Pharmaceutical and medicine mfg	3.0	5.1
5417	Scientific research and dev't	2.6	1.8
3341	Computer and peripheral mfg	2.1	-17.9
3364	Aerospace product and parts mfg	1.0	0.0
5413	Architecture and engineering	-0.4	2.8
5182	Data processing and hosting	-0.9	4.6
3345	Navigational, measuring, electro-medical,and control instr. mfg	-2.3	0.4
3344	Semiconductor, etc., mfg	-5.7	-6.6
3342	Communications equipment mfg	-5.9	-3.7

Figure 2.13 Percent change in the number of high-tech firms by industry in the United States, 2012–2014

Source: Small Business Dashboard, 2017.

The latest Global Entrepreneurship Monitor[10] 2016/17 (2017), an annual publication by the Global Entrepreneurship Research Association, incorporates data on 65 world economies. According to this report, the United States holds 24th rank among 65 countries in Total Entrepreneurial Activity (TEA)[11] (Figure 2.14).

According to GEC (2017), about 13 percent of the 326.6 million strong U.S population participates in TEA. The United States' high TEA

---

[10]The Global Entrepreneurship Monitor (GEM) is a global study conducted by a consortium of universities. It aims to analyze the level, patterns, trends, and dynamics of entrepreneurship occurring across multiple countries. It examines entrepreneurship through both surveys and interviews to field experts, conducted by the teams of each country. The main indicator used is called TEA (total early-stage entrepreneurial activity), which assesses the percentage of working age population that is about to start an entrepreneurial activity and that has started one from a maximum of 3 years and half. The report also looks into societal values and self-perceptions about entrepreneurship, phases/types of entrepreneurial activity, motivations for early-stage entrepreneurial activity, job creation projections, innovation, gender and age distribution of early-stage entrepreneurial activity, industry sector participation, the entrepreneurship ecosystem, etc.

[11]Global Entrepreneurship Monitor measures TEA rate as the percentage of the adult population (18 to 64 years) that is in the process of starting or who has just started a business. This indicator includes individuals who are participating in either of the two initial processes of the entrepreneurial process: nascent entrepreneurs—those who have committed resources to starting a business, but have not paid salaries or wages for more than three months—and new business owners—those who have moved beyond the nascent stage and have paid salaries and wages for more than three months but less than 42 months.

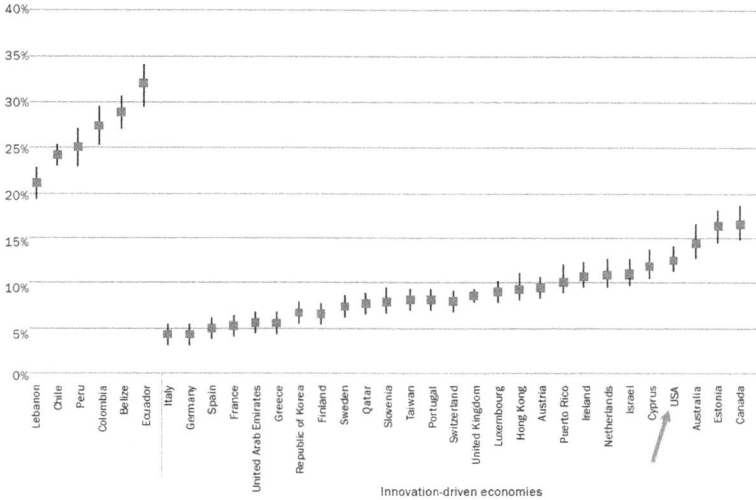

Figure 2.14 *Total early-stage entrepreneurial activity, the United States in the group of innovation-driven economies*

Source: Global Entrepreneurship Monitor. Global Report 2016-2017. 2017. file:///C:/Users/azhuplev/Downloads/gem-2016-2017-global-report-web-version-updated-210417-1492789938%20(2).pdf

level in the group of innovation-driven economies is surpassed by only three countries: Australia, Estonia, and Canada. The United States' latest country report (Global Enterprise Monitor 2015 Team, 2016) highlights some important trends in the state and dynamics of the entrepreneurial landscape in the country.

Opportunity perceptions among U.S. entrepreneurs dropped from a high of 51 percent in 2014 to 47 percent in 2015. This is the first drop since these perceptions began to rise in 2010. While the United States reports the highest level of capability perceptions (56 percent) at the innovation-driven development level, one-third of these economies report higher opportunity perceptions than the United States. This suggests that Americans remain highly confident in their abilities to start a business, but are seeing fewer opportunities to do so.[12]

---

[12]To some extent these dynamics might have been determined by the 2008 economic crises, the postcrisis economic revival, and the robust and improving state of the current U.S. economy, including its large corporate sector. With this, some people shift from their pursuit of entrepreneurial opportunities toward more predictable corporate jobs outside small business.

The United States reports the highest level of opportunity-motivated entrepreneurs who are improvement driven among the 24 innovation-driven economies. Sixty-nine percent of entrepreneurs in the United States stated that they were motivated to start by the pursuit of opportunity and desired to increase their income or the level of independence in their work. Nationally, 12 percent of Americans are leading and/or trying to start a social enterprise. On average, these enterprises engage a median number of seven paid workers and five volunteers. Although these entrepreneurs tap a variety of funding sources, government funding is the most popular source, revealing the importance of the government in helping entrepreneurs create social value. Entrepreneurship peaks among 35 to 44 year olds at 17 percent, and this age group is also most likely to engage in entrepreneurial employee activity. The high activity rates in this age group are accompanied by the highest levels of opportunity and capability perceptions as well as personally knowing an entrepreneur. Individuals in this age group are likely to have accumulated experience, credentials, relevant networks, and other resources they can leverage for their businesses. Workforce participation rates among the population aged 55 and older suggest that entrepreneurship, as well as established business ownership, is a key means of employment for those still working in their older years.

Age patterns in TEA rates by gender show low rates (7 to 9 percent) among younger women (18 to 34 years) and older women (45 to 64 years), with a spike upward to 15 percent in the middle (35 to 44 years) age group. Men maintain high rates throughout their working ages, declining substantially only after age 55. Additionally, while gender gaps exist in TEA rates, they are greater among established business owners and employee entrepreneurs, indicating the importance of looking across age groups, business phases, and contexts where this activity occurs.

Innovation levels among women dropped in 2015 to 32 percent of entrepreneurs, compared with 41 percent in 2014. This represents a reversal of a 4-year trend where women reported higher innovation rates than men. The decline in TEA rate was accompanied by reductions in impact indicators. Among a smaller number of entrepreneurs that were starting and running new businesses in 2015, fewer operated in the business services sector, and fewer expected to create six or more jobs in the next 5 years.

Job creation and profitability declined among established business owners: 22 percent added at least one job in the prior 2013 year, down from 27 percent in 2014. In 2015, 61 percent expected to be profitable, down from 91 percent in 2014. In 2015, 10 percent of entrepreneurs were starting businesses based on new technology, continuing a fluctuating but generally upward trend since hitting a low level of 4 percent in 2009. Entrepreneurs needed a median level of $17,500 to start their businesses in 2015, up from $15,000 three years prior, when finance questions were added to the 2012 survey. Financial requirements increased with greater job creation ambitions and for entrepreneurs in the extractive, transforming, and business services sectors. Entrepreneurs financed a dominant 57 percent of their funding needs themselves. Beyond personal sources, banks were the most popular funding source for entrepreneurs, with 36 percent of entrepreneurs stating that they used bank financing to start their business. Government sources also play an important role in business starts, providing funding to 22 percent of entrepreneurs. Crowdfunding, a still emerging source, contributed to the financial needs of 12 percent of entrepreneurs.

An in-depth examination of five states (California, Florida, New York, Ohio, and Texas) showed that New York and Ohio reported lower TEA rates than the U.S. national average. Contributors to these low rates include low opportunity motives among entrepreneurs, low activity among the middle age groups, and low and declining male participation in entrepreneurship.

While the United States tends to exhibit low international sales in general, the five states examined in depth all showed higher internationalization levels than the national average, with particularly high levels in Florida. This follows an increase in four of the states, while California declined from previously high levels (Global Enterprise Monitor 2015 Team, 2016).

Borrowing from e-commerce in its categorization of business formats, the most common of them are business-to-business (B2B), business-to-consumer (B2C), business-to-government (B2G), business-to-manager

(B2M), consumer-to-business (C2B), and consumer-to-consumer (C2C). Proliferation of these formats, their role, and prevalence in the United States mean different opportunities for companies of different types and sizes operating in different industries. From a foreign-based company's business perspective in the United States, deciding on whether it should target the end consumers (B2C), business customers (B2B), or customers in government agencies (B2G) depends on the company's background, current mission, size, business model, product/market positioning, current strategic posture, drivers and dynamics, business experience, and the scope of its presence in the United States, the host country.

The international trade and foreign direct investment landscape in the United States as measured in value (in dollar terms) is dominated by large corporations with a global outreach. In general, compared with SMEs, large corporations possess vast internal resources, market access, business expertise, access to outside financing, and management expertise and enjoy cost advantages from economies of scale. Large corporations in general are better positioned to compete by leveraging their power in strategic global presence and positioning and absorb the uncertainties and shocks of the start-up costs and risks in international expansion.

In general, foreign-based SMEs are not well positioned to partake in B2G and B2B commerce. Apart from competitive cost disadvantages against large corporations in the economies of scale, SMEs are often not capable of fulfilling sizeable orders and meeting logistical requirements needed for participation in government procurement programs and the big scope industrial supply chains. Government-imposed regulatory constraints, performance and reporting requirements, and possibility for negative customer perception effects of foreignness that overseas-based SMEs suffer from without having well-recognized brands may create strategic disadvantages for these companies.

Large-size foreign-based corporations can more effectively overcome some obstacles of doing business in the United States by leveraging their extensive financial resources, business expertise, brand power, and ability to sustain long-term presence in the host country. In contrast, small companies lacking these competitive advantages are often constrained in their business format largely to B2C only or, at best, can pursue B2B and B2G on a limited scale as part of their strategic alliances/joint ventures (JVs) with U.S.-based SMEs (Zhuplev, 2016b).

Business Start-up Logistics in the United States

As discussed in Chapter 1, due to dissimilarities in the critical impact factors and dynamics between the marketing-related and manufacturing-related overseas expansion alternatives, the approaches and logistics in these two forms of international business differ. A marketing-driven expansion tends to be simpler, less costly, and less risky than a manufacturing-driven expansion. In essence, a typical export transaction involves just logistics of goods and services characterized by shorter time frames, smaller financial commitments, and limited risks. In contrast, manufacturing-driven expansion may involve a sizeable long-term financial commitment for foreign direct investment; higher costs, liabilities, and risks; and complex logistics and management issues associated with expansion and operations in a host country.

Companies contemplating their international expansion in the U.S. market should weigh the following priorities:

- Is the contemplated expansion a good strategic fit with the company's background, organizational culture, and existing strategic mission?
- Does it enhance the company's strategic strengths and mitigate its weaknesses?
- Are there sufficient internal and external resources available for expansion?
- What are the short-term and long-term business benefits, costs, and risks associated with expansion? How do they balance against each other in the overall context? Do the benefits outweigh the costs and risks in the case of action versus no action?
- Which countries, markets, or global regions should be targeted in the first order of priority?
- What is the best entry mode/strategy for international expansion?
- Should the company expand early or late?
- Should the expansion be pursued on a small or large scale?

Some additional considerations may address further entrepreneurial start-up processes and dynamics, operational logistics, and growth in their entrepreneurial and managerial aspects, as well as strategies for steering the business through stages of growth, maturity, and eventually deciding on a possible market exit (Zhuplev, 2016a).

SMEs can find specific advice on doing business in the United States by reviewing government resources and manuals. For example, the USA. gov database contains a massive amount of useful information on doing business in the country.[13] Foreign government agencies responsible for trade promotion in English-speaking (e.g., Australia, Canada, or the United Kingdom) and other countries offer useful practical guides on various aspects of doing business in the United States (The Canadian Trade Commissioner Service, 2016; UK Trade & Investment, 2017a, b). Although these guides are designated for home-based small and medium size companies in those respective countries looking to do business in the United States, any entrepreneur or SME can access and take advantage of these resources.

For example, earlier, we discussed the Four Stages in Export Development (2017) framework (Figure 1.4) that outlines and integrates key stages (Build Export Capacity, Develop Export Markets, Make Sales/Get Paid, and Deliver the Goods) in the holistic export development process and recommends the necessary steps for each stage. In this context, a guide developed for Canadian businesses by the Canadian Trade Commissioner Service provides concise and yet reasonably comprehensive practical insights on priorities associated with export-related expansion to the United States. A synopsis of this guide, conveying the scope and topics covered in this export manual specifically tailored toward the United

---

[13]For instance, the section "State Business Resources" contains extensive information on small business in California. It includes detailed guidance and description of state government programs on opening a business: Start or Relocate a Business in California, Checklist for Starting a Business in California, California Secretary of State Business Programs; access to financing: Financing Startup Business in California, California Business Financing Portal, CA Business Portal State Incentives, Tax Credits and Funding; and contracting opportunities: Doing Business with the State of California, California eProcurement Portal & State Bid Opportunities, Federal Bid Opportunities in California (USA.gov, 2017).

States (for details see The Canadian Trade Commissioner Service, 2016), follows:

1. Before You Head South: The Canada–U.S. trade and economic relationship, Understanding Canada–U.S. relations, Understanding the North American Free Trade Agreement (NAFTA), Understanding the U.S. market, Market access issues, Global value chains and the U.S. market, Information sources for the U.S. market.

2. Preparing to Export to the United States: Is there a market for your company? Researching specific target markets, Assessing your company's readiness, Creating your export plan, Selecting your market, Developing your export marketing plan, Government services for exporters, Government training programs for U.S. bound exporters, Sourcing business opportunities.

3. Entering Your Chosen U.S. Market: Direct selling; Payments, returns, and warranties; Selling through intermediaries; Finding and checking out an intermediary; Working with your intermediary; Partnerships, investments, and acquisitions; U.S. government procurement; Market entry for service exports; Special issues for service exports (Cross-border movement of workers; Service exports and U.S. immigration classifications); Innovation: Science and technology exports.

4. The Legal Side of Exporting to the United States: NAFTA; Dealing with U.S. taxes; U.S. sanctions laws and regulations; Bribery and corruption legislation; Export contracts for goods; Export contracts for services; Obtaining contract insurance and bonding; Patents, trademarks, and copyrights; Protecting intellectual property from theft; Litigation in the United States; Product liability litigation.

5. The Basics of Export Financing: Types of financial assistance, Obtaining financial assistance, U.S. buyer financing, Payment methods, Dealing with nonpayment, Reducing financial risk through buyer credit checks, Reducing financial risk through export insurance, Currency fluctuations.

6. Business Travel to the United States: Documentation required for entering the United States, Entering the United States under NAFTA classifications (Business visitors, Professionals, Intra-company transferees,

Traders and investors), Entering the United States under non-NAFTA classifications, Travelling with samples and business gifts, Managing entry problems (Immigration issues for construction services, after-sales services, trade shows and sales staff, artists and craftspeople).

7. Labelling, Marking, and Standardization: Country of origin, Harmonized System (HS) codes, Technical regulations, standards and conformity assessment, Labelling and marking requirements of U.S. agencies (Federal Trade Commission [FTC], Food and Drug Administration [FDA], U.S. Department of Agriculture [USDA], Bureau of Alcohol, Tobacco, and Firearms and Explosives [ATF], Customs and Border Protection [CBP], Environmental Protection Agency [EPA], Consumer Products Safety Commission [CPSC], Department of Labor [DOL]).

8. Packing and Shipping Your Goods: Basic packing and shipping requirements; Shipping labels; Shipping methods; Reporting your exports; Controlled, prohibited, and regulated exports; Using freight forwarders; Insurance.

9. The Canada–U.S. Border: The Canada Border Services Agency, Canada–U.S. trusted trader programs, U.S. legislation affecting exporters.

10. Dealing with U.S. Customs: Customs brokers and what they do, Formal/commercial entry of goods, Required documentation for formal entry, Informal entry of goods, Clearing U.S. Customs, Duty deferral and duty relief, Penalties and seizures (The Canadian Trade Commissioner Service, 2016).

Keeping up with these multiple priorities and logistics in export-related expansion to the United States and the dynamic changes taking place in America's business environment and competitive marketplace, SMEs need to maintain a grasp of the big picture and megatrends. Euromonitor International publishes informative reports on multiple consumer and industrial markets, including its flagship "Consumer Lifestyles" report series. The latest Consumer Lifestyles in the United States (2017) report provides a wealth of useful market information and identifies the top five consumer trends in the United States.

Consumer Confidence Strong in an Improved Economy

A strong job market and rising incomes have been major factors behind American consumers' growing confidence. According to data published by the U.S. Labor Department, unemployment rates fell to 4.9 percent in October 2016 while U.S. Census Bureau data revealed that after years of stagnation, median household income increased by 5.2 percent in 2015, the highest growth since 2007. As a result, consumer spending, which accounts for nearly 70 percent of economic activity in the United States, has recorded considerable growth. In particular, there has been a significant increase in the demand for big-ticket items such as cars.

According to recent data released by the Conference Board, optimism about the economy hit a nine-year high in November 2016, with the group's consumer confidence index rising from 100.8 in October 2016 to 107.1 in November 2016. This increase appears to be consistent with an improving labor market and a solid growth in the consumer spending index, which has been at its highest since July 2007.

According to the recent data from the University of Michigan Survey of Consumers, consumer confidence is expected to continue its growth. "The latest reading indicates sentiment remains strong after President-elect Donald Trump's November victory, with Americans and businesses betting that tax cuts and looser regulation will help bring more opportunities for jobs and higher wages. At the same time, the survey showed a significant minority of respondents expected a negative impact from the new administration's policies, indicating a deep partisan divide over the outlook."

Record-Breaking Consumer Demand for Solar Energy

According to GTM Research and the Solar Energy Industries Association (SEIA), 7,286 MW of solar power was installed in 2015, an increase of 1,000 MW from 2014. SEIA believes that 2015 was a monumental year for the U.S. solar industry, which is poised to continue reaching unprecedented heights as our nation makes a shift toward a carbon-free source of energy that also serves as an economic and job-creating engine.

This increase was largely because of U.S. consumers warming up to solar energy. Tax credits, lower costs, and improved efficiencies have played a major role behind the growth in consumer demand, with more than one million homes having installed solar panels by 2016—in comparison to just 30,000 in 2006.

Consumers Making Healthier Choices

Greater public awareness of the health risks associated with obesity, combined with health campaigns and high health care costs, has prompted many consumers to question their lifestyle choices and seek healthier options. As a result, more U.S. consumers are incorporating exercise and recreational sports into their lives. Euromonitor's 2016 Global Consumer Trends survey results show that participation rates (at least once a week) in intensive physical activities such as yoga and dancing have increased from 30.6 percent in 2013 to 37.6 percent in 2016, while participation rates (at least once a week) in team sports have increased from 11 to 14.2 percent during the same time period.

At the same time, more consumers are moving away from dietary fads to healthier eating habits. One of the likely reasons behind this trend is that many people have become disillusioned with the various diets and programs. With each subsequent failure, people become more skeptical about the products. Some give up on losing weight altogether. As a result, Americans are increasingly *counting ingredients, not calories,* and avoiding heavily processed foods in favor of fresh and natural offerings. Consumers are looking to eat better and have become less concerned with counting carbohydrates, calories, or grams of fat. They are increasingly reading ingredients labels and are particularly interested in products that have a short list of ingredients they know and can pronounce.

Streaming Becomes Mainstream

According to an eMarketer report, 2016 was forecast to be the first time over half of the population watched digital TV. The report forecast that 50.8 percent of the population would watch TV shows online at least once a month, up from 47.8 percent in 2015. At the same time, a survey conducted by technology consulting firm Activate predicts that by 2020, 62 percent of consumers would subscribe to at least two streaming video applications. eMarketer's latest forecast of digital TV and movie viewership points to a growing embrace of over-the-top video, partly at the expense of traditional TV. This trend is driven by an expanding range of viewing devices, by favorable shifts in consumer behavior, and by a flood of new content from streaming services. Netflix, Amazon, and Hulu now compete elbow-to-elbow with TV networks and film studios for original programming. At the same time, consumers, especially Millennials, are increasingly using their smartphones to stream and watch movies and TV shows. According to Pew Research, the proportion of smartphone owners who used their phones to watch paid subscription services like Netflix and Hulu Plus has more than doubled in the past few years, increasing from 15 percent in 2012 to 33 percent in 2015. Younger Millennials, who came of age in the YouTube era, see digital video as a pervasive activity that cuts across genres and screens. They're among the heaviest users of smartphones and tablets, and they routinely use those devices—along with laptops and connected TVs—to watch everything from how-to clips, gaming streams, humor videos, and news blurbs to sports highlights, educational content, music clips, and scripted dramas.

The Sustainable Consumer

Sustainability is playing an increasingly important role when it comes to consumer purchasing behavior with 62 percent of online consumers stating that they tried to have a positive impact on the environment through their everyday actions, according to our survey results.

Additionally, according to the 2015 Tork Green Business Survey, 78 percent of consumers said that they purchased sustainable products and services, up from 75 percent in 2014. Furthermore, the survey found that 46 percent of Americans were willing to spend more money on products that were guaranteed to have followed ethical and responsible manufacturing practices, while 26 percent said that they knew if *green* claims were true or not on the basis of their own research. As consumers grow increasingly inclined to use their purchasing power toward environmentally sound products and services, the availability of and competition between these products will also increase. Brands and companies not only need to consider offering these products, if they do not already do so, but also need to seriously consider how they position the products and services in the marketplace, as that will impact their success.

At the same time, the 2015 Cone Communications Millennial CSR Study found that 91 percent of Millennials would switch brands if it were associated with a cause, in comparison with the U.S. average of 85 percent. Moreover, 66 percent used social media to engage around CSR[14] (versus 53 percent U.S. average). The report also states that Millennials are more enthusiastic in their support of corporate social and environmental efforts and are, above and beyond, more likely to say that they would participate in CSR initiatives if given the opportunity. Millennials are also prepared to make personal sacrifices to make an impact on issues they care about, whether that's paying more for a product, sharing products rather than buying, or taking a pay cut to work for a responsible company (Consumer lifestyles in the U.S., 2017).

References

Business Source Complete. 2017. https://www.ebsco.com/products/research-databases/business-source-complete

California Center for Jobs and the Economy. 2017. http://centerforjobs.org/california-fast-facts/#government

California Government. 2017. http://www.ca.gov/

The Canadian Trade Commissioner Service. 2016. "Exporting to the United States—A Guide for Canadian Businesses." http://tradecommissioner.gc.ca/exporting-to-united-states-exporter-aux-etats-unis.aspx?lang=eng

City of Carson. 2017. http://ci.carson.ca.us/ForBusinesses.aspx

Competitive Alternatives. 2016. KPMG. https://www.competitivealternatives.com/default.aspx

Consumer lifestyles in the U.S. 2017. Euromonitor International. http://www.euromonitor.com/consumer-lifestyles-in-the-us/report

County of Los Angeles. 2017. https://www.lacounty.gov/business

Doing Business. Measuring Business Regulations. 2017. The World Bank. http://www.doingbusiness.org/.

Doing Business 2017. 2017. Economy Profile 2017. United States. World Bank Group. http://www.doingbusiness.org/~/media/wbg/doingbusiness/documents/profiles/country/usa.pdf

---

[14]CSR stands for corporate social responsibility.

Driessen, M.P., and P.S. Zwart. 2010. "The role of the entrepreneur in small business success: the Entrepreneurship Scan" (PDF). http://www.ondernemerstest.nl/wp-content/uploads/2010/03/ICSBv5.pdf

Environmental Performance Index. 2017. http://epi.yale.edu/

Euromonitor International. 2017. https://www.researchandmarkets.com/s/euromonitor-international?gclid=CjwKCAjw3f3NBRBPEiwAiiHxGHW204XSbsSw5qvgjOkt5vf-WZnTJ2p19TeOy4ANgd_xVMaXTj8UiRoCijIQAvD_BwE

Export Development Canada. 2017. https://www.edc.ca/en/Pages/default.aspx

Global Competitiveness Report 2017–2018. 2017. http://www3.weforum.org/docs/GCR2017-2018/05FullReport/TheGlobalCompetitivenessReport2017%E2%80%932018.pdf

globalEDGE. 2017. https://globaledge.msu.edu/

Global Enterprise Monitor 2015 Team. 2016. "Global Entrepreneurship Monitor: 2015 United States Report." http://www.babson.edu/Academics/centers/blank-center/global-research/gem/Documents/GEM%20USA%202015.pdf

Global Entrepreneurship Monitor. 2017. Global Report 2016-2017. file:///C:/Users/azhuplev/Downloads/gem-2016-2017-global-report-web-version-updated-210417-1492789938.pdf.

GO-Biz. 2017. http://www.business.ca.gov/

Human Development Report. 2017. http://www.hdr.undp.org/en/2016-report

IBIS World. 2017. https://www.ibisworld.com/industry-trends/

Los Angeles Economic Development Corporation. 2017. https://laedc.org/research-analysis/latest-reports/

McKinsey Global Institute. 2017. http://www.mckinsey.com/mgi/overview

Milken Institute. 2017. http://www.milkeninstitute.org/centers/california/

Porter, M. 2012. California Competitiveness: Creating a State Economic Strategy. http://www.isc.hbs.edu/Documents/ced/states/State_Competitiveness---California_v312.pdf

Shobhit, S. 2017. "Entrepreneur vs. Small Business Owner." *Investopedia*. http://www.investopedia.com/articles/investing/092514/entrepreneur-vs-small-business-owner-defined.asp

SizeUp. 2017. https://www.sizeup.com/

Small Business Dashboard. 2017. https://smallbusiness.data.gov

Small Business Data Resources. 2017. https://www.sba.gov/sites/default/files/Small%20Business%20Data%20Resources%202013.pdf

Trading Economics. 2017. https://tradingeconomics.com/united-states/indicators

UK Trade & Investment. 2017a. "Establishing a Business Presence in the USA: UKTI Trade Services." https://www.gov.uk/government/uploads/system/uploads/attachment_data/file/301343/Establishing_a_Business_Presence_in_the_USA.pdf

UK Trade & Investment. 2017b. "Marketing in the USA: UKTI Trade Services." https://www.gov.uk/government/uploads/system/uploads/attachment_data/file/301339/Marketing_in_the_USA.pdf

University of Central Florida Libraries. 2017. Description of PEST/PESTLE analysis. http://guides.ucf.edu/industryanalysis/PESTLE

U.S. Small Business Administration. 2017. https://www.sba.gov/business-guide/plan/market-research-competitive-analysis

U.S. Small Business Administration: Office of Advocacy. 2017. https://www.sba.gov/sites/default/files/advocacy/SB-FAQ-2016_WEB.pdf

U.S. Country Profile. 2017. Euromonitor International. http://www.euromonitor.com/usa-country-profile/report

USA.gov. 2017. "Small Business in California." https://www.usa.gov/state-business/california

U.S. News & World Report. 2017. "Best States Rankings." https://www.usnews.com/news/best-states/rankings

World Competitiveness Yearbook. 2017. "IMD World Competitiveness Center." http://www.imd.org/wcc/world-competitiveness-center-rankings/world-competitiveness-yearbook-ranking/#WCY

World Factbook. 2017. https://www.cia.gov/library/publications/the-world-factbook/

World Happiness Report. 2017. http://worldhappiness.report/wp-content/uploads/sites/2/2017/03/HR17.pdf

World Trade Center, Los Angeles. 2017. https://www.wtcla.org/

Zhuplev, A. 2016a. *Doing Business in Russia: A Concise Guide*, Vol 1. New York, NY: Business Expert Press.

Zhuplev, A. 2016b. *Doing Business in Russia: A Concise Guide*, Vol 2. New York, NY: Business Expert Press.

CHAPTER 3

Market Entry

Strategy and Planning

We believed we could build a better search. We had a simple idea that not all pages are created equal. Some are more important.
—Sergey Brin (1974–present), a Russian-born American businessman, Google Cofounder

---

Main points in this chapter
- The marketer's uphill climb: be first, be better, or be different
- The American consumer: geography, generations, and diversity
- Understanding the market: your research toolbox

The Marketer's Uphill Climb: Be First, Be Better, or Be Different

It's incredibly difficult to persuade people to change their behavior and try new things. For instance, think about how difficult it is to simply persuade your (your kids, your spouse, your friends) to do something as simple as watching a new movie or trying a new restaurant. Behaviorally speaking, consumers (yes, you and me) are surprisingly irrational. Even when the benefits of a new product are clear as day, consumers often simply choose to stick with what they know and what products they have tried in the past. Behavioral economists Daniel Kahneman, Amos Tversky, and Richard Thaler have spent a lifetime researching and explaining why this is so. Long story short, people are *really* resistant to change. In examining this resistance to change, John Gourville, in his article "Why

Consumers Don't Buy: The Psychology of New Product Adoption," discusses a number of key behavioral insights into the decision-making process when it comes to evaluating new offerings:

1. *Compare to what they know:* People understand new product offerings in the context of a familiar reference point, also known as the status quo. This could be how a known product or service performs or how possessing it makes someone feel.
2. *Sensitive to gains and losses:* People will then compare the new product and consider what they might gain as well as what they might lose.
3. *Overvalue what they have:* People value items in their possession more than they value the same item not in their possession. (This is also known at the *endowment effect.*)
4. *Averse to losses:* People are more sensitive to losses rather than gains. In other words, giving something up hurts more than gaining something of equal value. Some research even indicates that losses are two to three times more painful than a gain of equal value.

A simple and relatable example is betting on a coin toss: The pain of losing $50 is far more substantial than the satisfaction of gaining $50. Keeping this in mind, when it comes to new product adoption, in order to drive behavior, *gains must outweigh losses.* Not an easy task in a heavily resourced country like the United States with countless and highly competitive offerings across industries. The role of marketing is central to meeting this challenge. The marketing discipline involves much more than simply crafting a clear message designed to highlight product/service advantages, although this is a very important piece of the puzzle. Truly effective marketing is about addressing consumer needs and wants, harnessing purpose, minimizing barriers, and providing *value* at each step of the customer journey—from information search to purchase and postpurchase assessment (e.g., Am I satisfied or not with my purchase?). The opportunities to deliver value are numerous as well as diverse—every message, video, website landing page, product package, shipping process, retail or customer service interaction, invoice and e-mail that you send is an opportunity to add value.

The value proposition[1] is especially important to SMEs with their own set of unique challenges: not enough money, time, resources, experience, and knowledge. The good news is that your competitors will make mistakes and markets and culture will constantly change—there is almost always room for one more smart and strategic player.

The smartest and most strategic players are often characterized by one (or more) of three areas in which they excel: They are (1) pioneers and first movers with respect to their industry or product, (2) better in terms of offering value through their product offering or cost structure, and (3) different and unique in terms of some element of their marketing mix. In the following sections, we explore specific frameworks, tools, tips, and approaches on how to stand out in the crowded and competitive U.S. market.

Be First, Be Better, or Be Different

When Volkswagen launched the Beetle stateside in 1959, they knew they had to make a splash by being different. At that time, the U.S. automotive landscape was saturated with huge American muscle cars from manufacturers like Buick, Ford, Pontiac, and Chevrolet. To enter the U.S. market, the iconic German automaker, with the help of its U.S. ad agency, Doyle Dane Bernbach (DDB), adopted the positioning of being different, in effect, highlighting how awesomely small the Beetle was as shown in Figure 3.1. Rather than making excuses for the Beetle's size or ignoring this seemingly disastrous positioning, Volkswagen bucked conventional wisdom and, as shown in the following print ad, embraced the diminutive nature of the Beetle.

Be First: A Lucky Strategy

Considering that there are 26 million small businesses registered in the United States, pioneering SMEs that are fortunate enough to have a

---

[1] A value proposition is a statement that clearly identifies what benefits a customer will receive by purchasing a particular product or service from a vendor.

Think small.

Our little car isn't so much of a novelty any more. A couple of dozen college kids don't try to squeeze inside it. The guy at the gas station doesn't ask where the gas goes. Nobody even stares at our shape. In fact, some people who drive our little

flivver don't even think 32 miles to the gallon is going any great guns. Or using five pints of oil instead of five quarts. Or never needing anti-freeze. Or racking up 40,000 miles on a set of tires. That's because once you get used to

some of our economies, you don't even think about them any more. Except when you squeeze into a small parking spot. Or renew your small insurance. Or pay a small repair bill. Or trade in your old VW for a new one. Think it over.

Figure 3.1 VW Beetle print ad created by Doyle Dane Bernbach (DDB) Advertising in 1959

truly unique offering that beats others to the mark and revolutionizes an industry should, first of all, give themselves a pat on the back. First-mover advantage offers myriad benefits, such as enabling a company to more easily gain strong brand recognition and customer loyalty before other market entrants arise, better control resources to make entry more difficult for others, and lock in relationships with retailers, distributors, and suppliers.

In 1979, the Japanese company Sony shocked the U.S. market when it launched its first-mover personal electronics product called the *Walkman*.

This handheld, portable cassette tape player revolutionized the music industry and went on to become one of Sony's most successful products ever, with almost 400 million units sold between 1979 and 2010. Not only had the Walkman name become synonymous with portable music, but competitors had a tough time keeping pace with Sony's rapid innovations from cassette to CD to MP3. The rapid success of the Apple iPod coupled with Apple's iTunes platform eventually ended the Walkman's 25-year reign.

Firms that successfully enter the U.S. market with a first-mover advantage face significant risks as well: fighting off domestic copycat products and services and protecting resources, processes, and intellectual property (IP) prior to and during market entry. Due diligence and a proper dose of caution and even paranoia go a long way as American businesses will move quickly to address and topple a new market entrant.

In his *Harvard Business Review* article,[2] Turkish businessman Hamdi Ulukaya talks about how he considered American yogurt disgusting—too sugary and watery—and because of this decided to make his own, just like how mother used to make it back on the family dairy farm in Turkey. It was serendipitous then when, in 2005, Hamdi learned of an old yogurt factory for sale in upstate New York. He jumped on the opportunity and quickly began crafting what today is known as Chobani Greek Yogurt. At the outset, with the help of only a few employees and no outside investors, he took great care to get the product and packaging just right—drawing from his previous overseas experiences with Greek yogurts—and made some very smart moves when it came to distribution, such as offering to pay retailer slotting fees (fees paid by brands to retailers for beneficial shelf space and placement in the store) over time versus paying them all at once (which he could not afford to do). Another crucial decision (and relevant to this point in the book) was to focus on the mass market grocery stores dairy aisle versus seeking to gain distribution among specialty stores. While Chobani wasn't the first Greek yogurt to enter the U.S. market, it was the first to break into the mainstream distribution channel consisting of national grocery store chains. At the time of Chobani's 2007 launch,

---

[2]https://hbr.org/2013/10/chobanis-founder-on-growing-a-start-up-without-outside-investors

Greek yogurt made up only 0.2 percent of the yogurt market share in the United States. Now it commands up 50 percent of total yogurt sales, and Chobani claims half of that.[3] In an interview with *Business Insider*, when talking about taking on the large U.S. multinational dairy players, Hamdi said, "I bet on these guys being lazy, that they're not going to wake up that fast, and I said, 'I'm going to be fast.'"[4]

Be Better: An Unlikely Strategy

Supposing you're not yet capable of turning an industry upside down or inventing an all-new category, the next step is to consider ways that you might be able to achieve a discernable competitive advantage. In other words, what can be done to make your product perceived as a better value versus the competition's? This is typically realized in one of two ways:

1. *Cost advantage: selling the same product or service for less than the competition's.* This can be accomplished either through pricing strategies (i.e., accepting smaller profit margins) or by reducing production costs through efficiencies in manufacturing. Many non-U.S.-based manufacturers are able to undercut manufacturing costs of American-made goods through less expensive materials and labor, thus offering their products at lower costs.
2. *Product advantage: providing a better product and/or service experience than a competitor's.* This can be achieved in a number of different ways, such as by offering superior customer service, faster shipping, shorter lines, better trained and/or friendlier staff, improved packaging, simpler payment terms and, of course, providing a superior product or service.

Here are a few companies that are really good at being better. When they were first starting out, many of America's most iconic companies simply focused on doing one thing better than everyone else. For example, online shoe retailer Zappos vowed to offer the best customer service, making it a part of their company DNA to "WOW" customers with

---

[3]http://www.businessinsider.com/the-success-story-of-chobani-yogurt-2013-5
[4]Ibid.

every interaction. Before Amazon became the juggernaut brand it is today, it simply focused on selling books and rose to power by systematically removing the pain-points of online shopping with fast shipping, one-click purchases, and thoughtful recommendations. Southern California burger maker In-N-Out rocked the fast-food world with never before seen quality, freshness, and friendliness. Starbucks offered a total experience, making it their mission to become "the third place" in consumers' lives between work and home.

After years of being perceived as producing low-quality cars with terrible designs, Korean auto manufacturer Hyundai Kia finally managed to convince the American consumer that their lower-priced vehicles are at par with the vehicles sold by Japanese manufacturers Honda and Toyota, both long-known for their dependability, reliability, and quality. Today, most Hyundai Kia products are seen as well designed and packed with the latest technology; yet, they remain priced several thousand dollars less than their Japanese and American rivals. That said, even a deep discount on a quality product isn't enough to tip the scales. If you recall the note about marketer's uphill climb—essentially how difficult it is to get consumers to change their behavior—in addition to lower price, nice design, and at-par quality, Hyundai Kia needed to offer a far better warranty in order to convince consumers to give their vehicles a try: a 10-year/100,000-mile warranty compared with Honda's 5-year/60,000-mile warranty. The strategy is working though, as Hyundai Kia has enjoyed consistent year-over-year growth, and in 2016 the Kia brand celebrated its best ever annual sales.

Non-U.S. (foreign) companies can also benefit greatly from their country of origin's positive associations and perceptions. For example, Americans tend to believe that Swiss watches are more precise, German cars are more luxurious, Japanese electronics are more durable, Italian fashion is more cutting edge, and Swedish furniture is more intelligently designed. Simply leveraging a business's country of origin can signal powerful attributes and benefits to the consumer without having to do much explaining at all. When MontGras Chilean wines was preparing to launch their products in the United States, the company decided to envelop the brand in its inherent "Chilean-ness." Doing so not only gave MontGras a wonderful local story to tell, but it also immediately distinguished it from every other wine in the aisle. Copy from the website emphasized the country-of-origin effect:

> Founded in 1998, Ninquén, meaning "Plateau on a Mountain" in a native dialect, became Chile's first Mountain Vineyard. This inimitable terroir, located in the heart of Colchagua—Chile's most renowned premium winemaking region—provides exceptional grape growing conditions for the production of ultra-premium red wines. MontGras was a midsized winery when it first launched in the U.S., now it is among one of the largest in the country.

Be Different: A Likely Strategy

Marketing thought leader and author Al Ries claims, "It's better to be different than to be better."[2] In most categories, consumers can predictably be expected to default to the #1 or #2 leading brand. They often assume that the most recognized and well-known brands are also the best. Social science calls this the *bandwagon effect*—if everyone else is doing it, it must be the best, right? Maybe, maybe not. Being better hardly matters when consumer preference is so strongly tied to perceptions. For most SMEs and new market entrants, it's almost impossible to beat the market share leaders at their own game. After all, these market leaders have more experience, more resources, more capital, more people, more partners, and frankly, greater levels of consumer trust. That's where being different comes in, and in most cases, being different is much more doable than being better.

READER BEWARE! There's a deadly space that many marketers find themselves in called the *mushy middle*. It's the place where the brand, product, or service is neither the best nor the cheapest nor is it notably different in the consumer's mind. It's critical that you are known for, and stand for, something. Fortunately, there are a variety of simple (but not always easy) ways to add value, create positive perceptions, and ultimately differentiate yourself without having to rely on discernable price and product advantages:

> *Embrace your country of origin:* For many foreign SMEs, one of the simplest ways to differentiate is to tell your country-of-origin story.

This is especially true if your country of origin already has positive associations that you can leverage. For example, Germany is known for engineering, Switzerland for precision and craftsmanship, Mexico for textiles, and so on.

Have personality: People, especially Americans, love people and brands that have personality. This is not only a helpful tool for differentiation, it is also essential to capturing attention in a country such as the United States where the average person's attention span is 8 seconds (less than a goldfish, apparently).

Break the category rules: Research your category in an attempt to identify standard industry conventions. For instance, what are the design elements that your competitors tend to use—color, typeface, packaging, size? Once you know, disrupt them. Be the transparent brand in a category of mistrust, or the simple brand in a world of complexity. For example, bottled water is almost always sold in plastic bottles. The Boxed Water brand disrupted the category by providing water in a box. The electronics category tends to be feature driven with very sales-oriented packaging and boxy, generic-looking designs. Apple disrupted the industry with a clean and modern look. For a hundred years the traveling circus was about freaks and misfits. The Canadian company Cirque de Soleil made it about art and beauty.

Create an Experience: In his book *The Experience Economy*, author Joseph Pine makes the case that, as markets become more crowded and competition becomes fiercer, products and services that once possessed a solid competitive advantage risk becoming commoditized and commanding low margins, take Figure 3.2, for example, coffee: In its raw form, coffee is a commodity, worth a few cents per pound, but by simply roasting, packaging, and adding a name to it, it becomes a consumer good and commands a few dollars per pound. That said, there are hundreds if not thousands of coffee brands and thousands of places to get a cup of coffee in the United States. Some of these brands even add a service component to their product: They brew and serve it to customers commanding a dollar or more per cup, or in the case of a restaurant in New York City,

$24 per cup! Taking a commodity such as coffee and building an experience around the brand is why Starbucks has become "the third place" regardless of where in the world the consumer might be. Because of its ability to create a consistent and familiar experience, Starbucks has not only established a dominant position in the market, but is also able to charge a premium for each cup of coffee it serves.

Make life better, even just a little bit: In a market where nearly 7 in 10 consumers agree with the statement, "Businesses bear as much responsibility as governments for driving social change,"[5] it makes sense that purpose-driven brands like TOMS, Tesla, Facebook, and Google are by and large the leading choice among consumers. Purpose-driven brands tend to perform better, so much so that we discuss this topic in greater detail in Chapter 4. Here's the good news though: You don't need to change the world in order to reap the benefits; just try to make life a little better than it was before you entered your consumer's world.

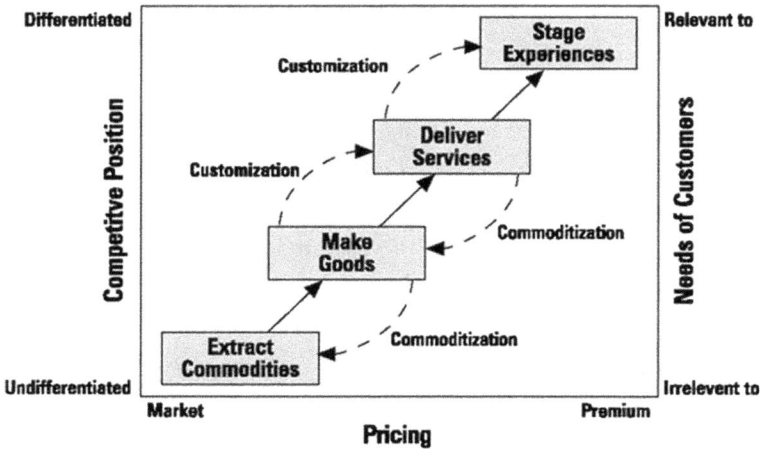

Figure 3.2 Graphic from Joseph Pine and James Gilmore's book, The Experience Economy, *1999*

---

[5]https://www.campaignlive.com/article/brands-not-government-drive-social-change-say-consumers-study/1380448

Be True to Your Brand

A case for staying true to your roots: The last thing that the American fashion retail market needed in the late 2000s was another fast-fashion retailer (e.g., low cost, huge variety). Aside from the United States being in a recession with record-high unemployment and a struggling retail industry, the American fashion market was saturated with large-scale clothing manufacturers like H&M, Zara, Forever 21, Gap, Old Navy, Banana Republic, Abercrombie & Fitch, and more. Amidst all of this competition, there was an empty space in the U.S. market for an authentic British clothing brand. Enter Topshop/Topman. Well-known throughout Europe and with a significant presence in England, the British company launched their first stateside store in New York City in 2009. Their U.S. presence has since grown to nearly 100 coast-to-coast locations, garnering a presence in nearly every major U.S. market. Topshop/Topman's "UK-ness" wasn't necessarily perceived as a product benefit as there was nothing inherently better about UK fashion or Topshop's offerings; it was simply perceived as different—offering U.S. shoppers an all-new angle on style and retail experience.

Questions to Consider

- Do you have a clear competitive advantage versus the competition? If so, what is your value proposition? If not, what are some ways in which you can simply *be different?*
- What kind of experience, beyond the product itself, does your brand offer? In thinking about your competitors' marketplace offerings, is that sufficient to be competitive? What else could you do to increase your overall value proposition?
- What are the American consumers' perceptions of your country (the country-of-origin effect)? Is this an element that could be and should be leveraged in your marketing?

The American Consumer: Geography, Generations, and Diversity

We still believe in the America that is the land of opportunity and a beacon of freedom. We believe in the America that challenges each of us to be better and bigger than ourselves.

—Mitt Romney (1947–present), 2012 U.S. Presidential Nominee, from New Hampshire primary speech

Considering the time line of world civilizations, the United States is very much a young country. Founded on July 4, 1776, as the Declaration of Independence was signed, the country has remained a beacon to many of the world's emigrants seeking a better way of life. This desire for opportunity and progress and the founding vision for freedom, equality, and democracy are interwoven into the very fabric of American society and drive the core values that nearly all American's share, such as diversity, individualism, competition, achievement, and success. While American values are the glue that unifies its people, there are also many diverse Americas. The vast differences among the millions of inhabitants of the United States significantly impact how American consumers shop, purchase, and consume goods as well as media. Although these differences can be sliced, diced, and explained in myriad ways, this chapter will focus on two key drivers: American lifestyles and generational cohorts. Before we examine American lifestyles and cohorts (what we will refer to as *market segments*), however, it is important to understand the geography of the United States.

U.S. Geography

With a population of nearly 330 million people, the United States is the third most populous country in the world. However, with a land mass of nearly 3.8 million square miles (9.8 million square meters), the United States ranks 79th in terms of population density when compared with the top 100 most populous countries in the world.[6] The United States consists of 50 states, containing over 3,000 municipal counties and nearly

---

[6]https://en.wikipedia.org/wiki/List_of_countries_and_territories_by_population_density

20,000 incorporated areas such as cities and towns.[7] Of these towns and cities, there are approximately 285 cities with populations over 100,000. Each state, county, city, town, and neighborhood has their own unique characteristics when it comes to demographics such as age, income, employment, and education as well as consumer psychographics like attitudes, opinions, and beliefs. For instance, Manhattan Beach (an affluent coastal city in Southern California) is vastly different from a city like Ferndale, Michigan (a middle-city outside of Detroit with a deep history tied to the U.S. automotive industry). These variances, of course, amount to differences in preferences and behaviors when it comes to consumer behavior (e.g., shopping and purchase habits). Granted the digital media and online shopping revolution coupled with an extensive interstate freeway distribution network has toppled many of these divisions and made the United States a more horizontal mass market; however, our objective is to provide road maps and tools to aid in selecting those key markets in which to establish your U.S. presence.

As Figure 3.3 indicates, the population (and income) density in the United States is disproportionately distributed along the region's coasts. For this reason, the United States is often thought of in terms of the East and West coasts and everything else in between (sometimes referred to as the Heartland, essentially the area consisting of 26 states with primarily suburban and rural communities sandwiched between the populous urban coasts).

The U.S. census department divides up the country into four major parts: West, Midwest, Northeast, and South (see Figure 3.4). Each of these regions, while far from homogenous, contains many similarities in terms of geography, weather, mind-set, culture, politics, and more. Major cities within these geographic areas include cities in the Northeast (Boston, New York, Philadelphia), the South (Atlanta, Orlando, Miami, Dallas, Houston), the Midwest (Chicago, Detroit, Indianapolis, St. Louis), and the West (Los Angeles, San Francisco, Phoenix, Las Vegas, Seattle, and Portland). Rural areas in the United States account for 97 percent of the country's land yet only 20 percent of the population.[8]

---

[7] https://www.census.gov/content/dam/Census/library/publications/2015/demo/p25-1142.pdf

[8] https://www.census.gov/newsroom/press-releases/2016/cb16-210.html

Population density, 2010

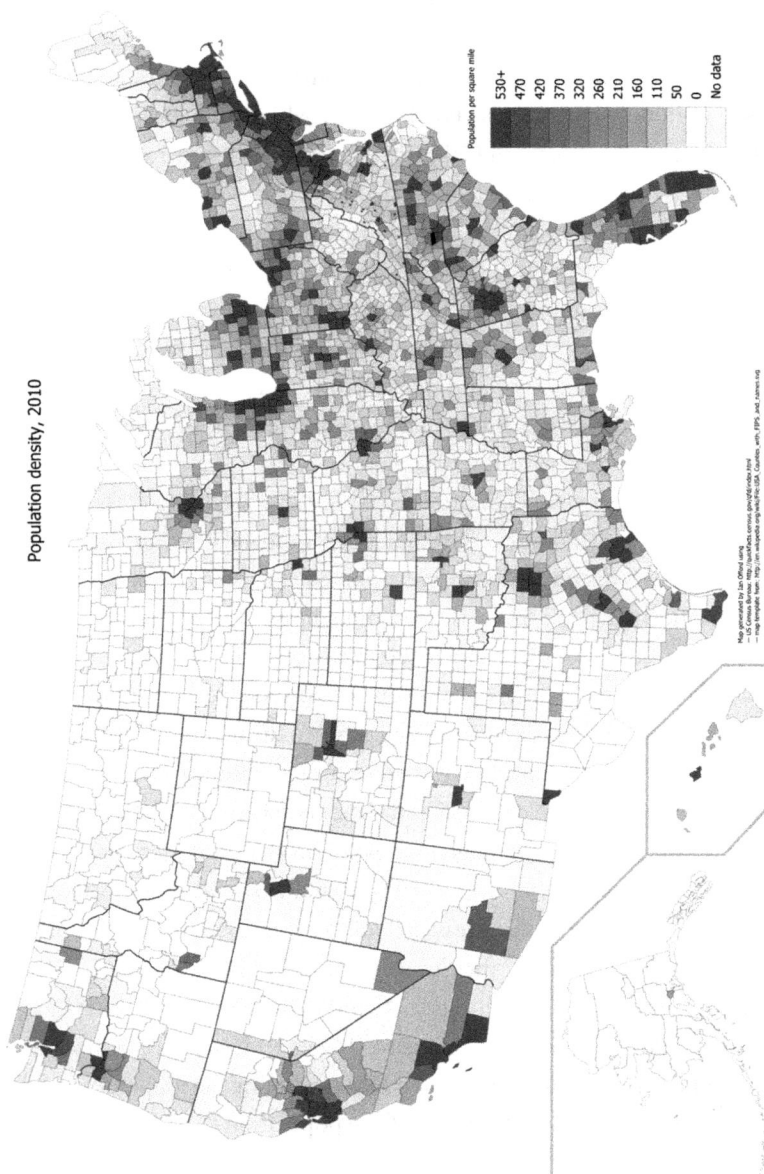

Population per square mile

530+
470
420
370
320
260
210
160
110
50
0
No data

Map generated by Ian DHied using
— US Census Bureau http://quickfacts.census.gov/qfd/index.html
— US Census Bureau, Counties, with, FIPS, and, names svg
— map template from http://en.wikipedia.org/wiki/File:USA_Counties_with_FIPS_and_names.svg

Figure 3.3 Population density map, 2010

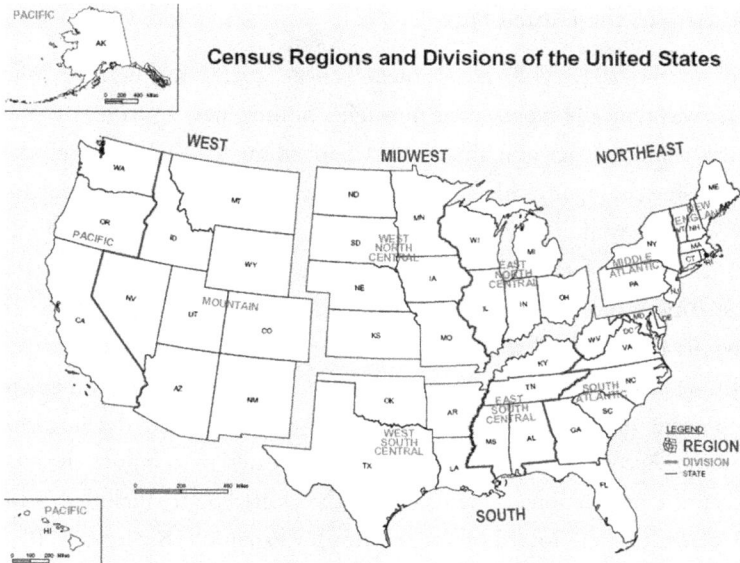

Figure 3.4 Census regions map

The Western United States, specifically California, Oregon, and Washington, is generally viewed as liberal, easy going, progressive, and open minded. People living within these states, particularly urban markets in California, are also characterized as being influenced by subcultures such as surfing and skateboarding. The Midwest is often described as "salt of the earth," full of hard-working people with family-oriented values. The Midwest region, however, has struggled more in recent decades due to the decline in heavy manufacturing like steel and automotive, and some cities in the Midwest, such as Detroit, are in the process of reinventing themselves in a postrecession United States. The South is known for its "southern hospitality," with an ultra-friendly attitude, conservative values, and high rates of religion. The South, however, is sometimes characterized as being closed minded when it comes to diversity and inclusion (a perception dating back to the days of slavery in the United States). Lastly, the Northeast is known for its high-intellect, fast-paced urban living and direct, in-your-face attitude (Northeasters are sometimes viewed as curt or rude). Of course, as with any generalization or stereotype, while it may characterize a large population, it is hardly an accurate depiction of specific individuals within the market.

Diversity in the United States

Prior to the 2010 U.S. government census, marketing in the United States was typically represented through a homogeneous, primarily white America and the face of mainstream American media—its actors, models, newscasters, company chiefs, advertising executives—were disproportionally white as well. The 2010 census report and subsequent data revealed the new truth related to American demography—that, for the first time, most American children under the age of five are no longer white. The previous minority (Hispanic, Black, Asian, and multicultural individuals) now represents the majority. This is in contrast to the fact that only 14 percent of Americans over the age of 85 fall within the nonwhite minority. According to a 2016 Kaiser Family Foundation report, the racial and ethnic population segments within the United States included White (61 percent of the total U.S. population), Hispanic (18 percent), Black (12 percent), Asian (6 percent), and Other (3 percent). In fact, 80 percent of the U.S. population growth through 2020 will come from minorities, with over half of this growth coming from Hispanic Americans.[9] A 2017 MediaPost Research Brief also noted that the almost 60 million Hispanic Americans represent $1.5 trillion in purchasing power.[6]

In parallel with this demographic shift, long-held and deeply ingrained symbols of American culinary life such as hamburgers, ketchup, and potato chips are suddenly being challenged by new cultural influences. Salsa has overtaken ketchup as the #1 condiment sold in the United States, tortilla chips are outselling potato chips, and tacos and burritos have replaced hamburgers at the dinner table.[10] Apart from food, in 2012, 81 percent of the Billboard Top 10 best-selling albums were from nonwhite or mixed-race groups of artists.[11]

---

[9]Hispanic Millennials in America article from MediaPost Research Brief: https://www.mediapost.com/publications/article/306819/42-of-millennials-are-multicultural.html?utm_source=newsletter&utm_medium=email&utm_content=headline&utm_campaign=104997&hashid=Ener-2NxZNUeNxwxxCfClWiVs9I

[10]http://www.foxnews.com/food-drink/2013/10/17/salsa-outsells-ketchup-as-american-tastes-change.html

[11]http://www.businessinsider.com/charts-white-people-are-no-longer-relevant-in-pop-music-in-terms-of-sales-2012-3

Nielsen, a leading media-measurement research provider, divides the United States into what it calls designated marketing areas (DMAs). DMAs are defined as an exclusive geographic area consisting of counties in which the local market television stations hold a dominance of the total hours viewed. Nielsen has sliced the United States into 210 DMAs, all of which measure viewership behaviors. Figure 3.5 highlights a map that illustrates population composition in DMAs by ethnicity. Not surprisingly, nonwhite millennial minority groups such as Hispanics, African American, and Asian tend to gravitate toward the coasts and major cities.

It's not a secret that there is a relationship between ethnicity, brand and product category perception, and media and consumption behaviors. Take, for example, Apple's iPhone iOS versus Google's Android operating system (OS) adoption. Looking at a map of iOS installs in Los Angeles, it becomes clear that the coastal and northern areas (primarily white) choose iOS and the south and central parts of the city (primarily African American and Hispanic) prefer Android.

U.S. Generational Cohorts

Cutting across geography and ethnicity, however, lies what we refer to as *generational cohorts,* groups of individuals whose behaviors and influences are defined by the generations in which they were born and raised. A *generation* can be defined as a group of people born around the same time who are raised in the same place, and research has shown that people in a similar *birth cohort* demonstrate similar characteristics, behaviors, preferences, and values over their lifetime.[12] A primary driver of the formation of cohort mind-sets includes key shared experiences of the group that shape their values, aspirations and attitudes. Insight from generational cohorts can be used to develop products, plan and develop media strategy, create advertising messaging, and identify workplace opportunities. Generations also tend to contain important life-stage opportunities, or moments in which people are more open to purchase, such as when entering college, landing that first job, buying a house, starting a family, or beginning retirement. Figure 3.6 highlights and compares relevant attributes by cohort.

---

[12]The Center for Generational Kinetics.

Figure 3.5 *Top 10 multicultural millennial DMAs*

Source: http://santiagosolutionsgroup.com/wp-content/uploads/2017/01/Top-10-Multicultural-DMA_ver01-23-17Final.pdf

The figure contains the following content:

TOP 10 MULTICULTURAL MILLENNIALS DMAs

SANTIAGO SOLUTIONS GROUP

9 of the 10 Top 10 Multicultural (MC) Millennial DMAs are among the Top 10 Overall Millennial DMAs in the U.S. Of the Top 10 MC DMAs, 6 rank among the Top 10 Hispanic Millennial DMAs, 8 rank among the Top 10 African American DMAs and 7 rank among the Top 10 Asian/Other DMAs. NY, LA, Chicago and Houston are the most diverse DMAs, ranking on the Top 10 for all Multicultural segments.

Share of Segment in DMA*

Top DMA — Ranked by Overall Millennial Population	Hisp Mill.	Af.Am. Mill.	Asian/O Mill.	M/C Millennials
New York	25%	19%	10%	54%
Los Angeles	48%	8%	11%	67%
Chicago	22%	20%	6%	48%
Dallas-Ft.Worth	33%	14%	4%	52%
Philadelphia	13%	19%	8%	40%
S.Francisco-Oak-S.Jose	25%	7%	33%	65%
Houston	40%	12%	6%	59%
Washington D.C.	17%	20%	17%	54%
Atlanta	15%	30%	6%	51%
Boston	10%	6%	7%	23%
Phoenix	32%	3%	7%	42%
Seattle-Tacoma	13%	4%	18%	35%
Miami-Ft. Lauderdale	61%	13%	2%	75%
Detroit	5%	21%	7%	33%
Sacramnto-Stkton	30%	9%	20%	58%
San Diego	38%	5%	13%	56%
Raleigh-Durham	12%	31%	13%	50%
San Antonio	60%	4%	3%	67%

Legend:
- Multicultural Top 10
- Hispanic Top 10
- African Am. Top 10
- Asian/Other Top 10

Source: SSG analysis of GfK MRI Market-to-Market 2015
©2017 Santiago Solutions Group,Inc. SantiagoSolutionsGroup.com
(818) 509-5901 Carlos@santiagosolutionsgroup.com

Characteristics	Depression cohort (pre–1946)	Baby boomer cohort (1946–1964)	Generation X cohort (1965–1981)	Generation Y cohort (1982–1995)	Generation Z cohort (born after 1995)
Formative experiences	The great depression/world war II/defined gender roles/nuclear families/sense of duty and patriotism	The cold war/Vietnam/space travel/rock and roll/the hippy movement	The Reagan era/AIDS epidemic/intro of PCs/early mobile phones/punk rock/Internet's emergence	Apple (iPod, iPad, iPhone)/laptops/PlayStation/social media (MySpace, Facebook)	Threat of global warming/terrorism/mobile devices/social media (Snapchat, Instagram)
Aspiration	Long-term career/home and car ownership	Job security/home and car ownership	Work-Life balance	Independence/mobility/rapid career advancement	Driven by social causes/start-up mentality
Views on technology	Skeptical/late adopters	Early adopters	Internet pioneers	Internet savvy	Digital natives/born on the Internet
Views toward career	Life-long employers	Strivers/organizational climbers	Value career over the organization	Have digital skills, will travel	Remains to be seen
Defining product	Homes	Homes/cars/televisions/computers	Personal computers/video games	Anything apple	Airbnb/Uber/Lyft
Favored media	Television, radio/newspaper	Television/radio/magazines	Television, Internet	Social media/online streaming/Instagram/	Social media/YouTube
Communication preference	Phone/face-to-face	Phone/voice mail/e-mail	Phone/SMS/e-mail	E-mail/social media/SMS	Social media/SMS

Figure 3.6 Characteristics and attributes by generational cohort

Source: Compiled from http://www.businessinsider.com/definition-of-generational-cohorts-2013-5 and https://wealth.barclays.com/global-stock-and-rewards/en_gb/home/research-centre/talking-about-my-generation.html.

Key Trends Shaping the Marketing Landscape

An example of the value of uncovering and monitoring trends includes the trade publication *Adweek* and its recent report of a study by Defy Media of the Gen Z cohort. The findings reveal a significant shift in attitudes and behaviors among this cohort relative to those that preceded it. For example, nearly all of Gen Z report to use YouTube regularly. Gen Z individuals are also more apt to trust social media celebrities than more mainstream celebrities. Finally, a majority of Gen Z consumers find celebrity-promoted content (i.e., a new face cream promoted by Kim Kardashian) acceptable, even appealing, as a form of advertising.

At a national level, demographic cohort trends help to paint a picture of a United States in transition.[13] First, the number of homeowners in the United States peaked in 2006 and has fallen since. Second, the annual birth rate in the United States has declined since 2007 and the number of marriages among Millennials is falling as well. Third, urban centers are growing and rural areas declining in terms of population. Fourth, the income gap in the United States continues to widen.[14] By 2015, the top 1 percent of Americans in terms of income will average 40 times that of the bottom 90 percent.

Taken together, there are two key trends that help define the U.S. consumer across cohort and ethnicity. First, old or young, individuals in the United States increasingly exhibit what we call an *on-demand* mind-set of wanting the media content that they want now (e.g., entertainment, sports, news). This need for immediacy is also apparent in the U.S. retail industry with online retailers such as Amazon now focusing on timely (1 day) order fulfillment as a key driver of their business model. The quest for convenience is also a major influence on the U.S. consumer. Whether it be transportation services such as Uber or Lyft, food-on-demand services such as Door Dash, or one-click purchasing using Amazon Prime, the U.S. consumer simply hates to wait.

Interestingly, although online shopping behavior has become a common practice coast to coast, many U.S. consumers still prefer the option of visiting brick-and-mortar retail spaces, primarily because of the ability to see, touch, and try on the product as well as experience the gratification

---

[13]https://www.mediapost.com/publications/article/306364/behind-the-headlines-in-the-21st-century.html

[14]https://inequality.org/facts/income-inequality/

of immediate possession. We also see a return to physical retail for brands seeking to establish a brand *experience* for consumers through retail show-cases. For example, the eyewear brand Warby Parker operates storefronts that serve as physical try-on locations to supplement its online presence and to help consumers order its eyewear online, and the shoe brand TOMS has opened flagship stores in key markets such as Los Angeles, Amsterdam, and London to showcase not only TOMS products but its One-for-One Giving Program as well. Interestingly, motivations for physical stores show slight variance by region: For urban coastal consumers, preference toward physical spaces is driven more by the social aspects and increased selection (urban areas tend to have large, well-designed shopping centers with a wide variety of stores and restaurants), whereas those in the more suburban and rural areas prefer physical spaces and retailers such as Walmart more for their low prices and convenience. It's also important to note that urban and suburban consumers tend to place more value on (and pay more for) well-known brand names whereas rural consumers are driven more by cost savings.[15]

Questions to Consider

- In thinking about your possibilities for targeting, messaging, media selection, pricing, and distribution, what are implications of the U.S. geographic, ethnic, and generational differences on your analysis?
- What are the pros and cons of focusing your efforts on a specific region and/or cohort?
- Conversely, what steps could be taken to help you achieve broad appeal while taking these vast differences into account?

Understanding the Market: Your Research Toolbox

The right question is usually more important than the right answer to the wrong question.
        —Alvin Toffler (1928–2006), American businessman, writer,
                and futurist, from the book *The Third Wave*.

---

[15]https://www.mediapost.com/publications/article/301540/shopping-behavior-in-the-heartlands.html?utm_source=newsletter&utm_medium=email&utm_content=headline&utm_campaign=103267&hashid=Ener-2NxZNUeNxwxxCfClWiVs9I

Today's marketing landscape is vast, with a seemingly infinite number of agencies, consultants, companies, and brands all making decisions employing a seemingly endless supply of information and data. Marketing decision making is a difficult process, involving evaluating countless variations on marketing strategy and tactics that can help companies to define and reach their specific target markets more efficiently and effectively. Developing and adhering to a marketing strategy and plan is also a major challenge, and it is more so without a road map. That's where understanding your market through market research comes in—it helps organizations to collect and make sense of data regarding their marketing mix—the product, pricing, promotions, and distribution plans—in order to execute, measure the effectiveness of, and optimize marketing strategy and tactics.

Looking back, the 1980s in America were a decade defined by Punk Rock, Madonna, Jane Fonda and the Aerobics craze, and, particularly relevant to this chapter, *The Cola Wars*. Throughout the 70s and into the early 80s, the soft drink brand Pepsi had been taking market share slowly but surely from the venerable American brand Coca-Cola. Pepsi was aggressively attacking Coca-Cola's flagship Coke brand in the United States with strategies and campaigns such as The Pepsi Challenge, and by 1984 Coca-Cola had lost 1 percent of its market share while Pepsi had gained one and half percentage points.[16] Advertising and distribution efforts by Coke did nothing to stem the decline. Therefore, the smart and savvy executives at Coca-Cola headquarters in Atlanta decided that they needed to do something drastic, and fast. The company dedicated 2 years and millions of dollars in conducting research, including thousands of focus groups, interviews, and blind taste tests. What it found was that consumers seemed to prefer the sweeter taste of Pepsi over Coke. In response, Coca-Cola completely removed Coke from store shelves and vending machines and replaced it with what it called New Coke. Within minutes of the launch (and the demise of the original Coke), New Coke became news, but not the kind of news Coca-Cola was aiming for. Months after thousands of complaints along with daily negative press reports and articles flooded the company's headquarters, Coca-Cola reversed course

---

[16]"Introducing New Coke" HBS Case 9-500-067 Susan Fournier.

and reintroduced its flagship Coke brand. The lesson learned? Although the quantitative research behind the New Coke launch was accurate, the myopic strategy to replace original Coke failed to consider the history and emotional connection behind the Coke consumption experience, especially among loyal consumers. Sweeter taste or not, loyal Coke drinkers wanted their original Coke back.

The lesson here is that actionable research is part science, part art, and part intuition. That said, there are two things that increase your odds of uncovering true and insightful results: thoroughness and an open mind. There is a concept in behavioral psychology called *confirmation bias*—we basically can, and will, find what we believe to be true, to be true. We will, subconsciously, confirm our suspicions by ignoring contrary evidence and instead focusing on the data that support our needs. With this in mind, the following frameworks, approaches, and tools have been selected to help guide you in a thorough and systematic analysis of your potential business opportunity in the complex U.S. market and at the same time help you uncover those valuable insights and avoid the threat of confirmation bias.

Situational Analysis

The first step in developing new products and entering new markets is to gather intelligence from a multitude of sources and viewpoints. This is where Coca-Cola failed in its market research. Market intelligence gathering typically begins with a deep situational analysis, which can be based on both secondary data (data that are collected and generated by external, third-party firms) and primary data (data collected and generated by your organization). In terms of secondary data, there are thousands of free or inexpensive secondary online resources available and that are at your fingertips, a Google search away. At times, however, you may need to ask questions and conduct research for which there are simply no answers available from secondary data. In these instances, companies conduct their own primary research or commission custom research from a reputable market research vendor or partner. Further, there are a host of free and cost-effective self-service tools that you can access to help in the search of a market research vendor. For example, the GreenBook

Directory (www.greenbook.org) provides a comprehensive list of market research providers organized by specialty.

4Cs and SWOT Analysis Frameworks

When identifying your research needs and forming your research plan, it is important for companies of all sizes, especially SMEs, to systematize and organize their research. For this, we propose two basic and valuable frameworks: (1) the 4Cs (Figure 3.7) and (2) SWOT (Figure 3.8) analyses.

The 4Cs help companies to better understand the current and historical trends affecting the company and its performance, the category (often referred to as industry), the competitive set, and the consumer or customer.

After completing the 4Cs framework, the next step is to summarize and organize the findings uncovered in your 4Cs situational analysis to generate insights, identify roadblocks, and determine action items. This is accomplished by employing the framework called a SWOT that was introduced in Part One of this book—a systematic accounting of internal Strengths and Weaknesses as well as external Opportunities and Threats.

An important distinction with the SWOT analysis is that it guides the marketer to identify which elements are within the firm's direct control (internal factors) and which are not (external factors). Elements that are in the firm's control include target selection and the marketing mix (product, promotions, pricing, and distribution). Factors over which the firm does not have direct control must be either seized as opportunities or identified, mitigated, or overcome as threats. However, it is important to note that in a SWOT analysis there is an inherent *connection* between the internal and external factors. In other words, what companies do to address strengths and weaknesses can also affect related opportunities and threats.

In 1996, when Russian-born Sergey Brin was working toward his PhD at Stanford University in California, he saw an opportunity: As worldwide Internet users were doubling each year, the available search engine options were underwhelming. Capitalizing on this, he and fellow doctoral student Larry Page created an online search tool—that ranked pages on the basis of importance—called BackRub, which later became known as Google.

Company
- Product history
- Short- and long-term business/sales/communication objectives
- Historical advertising/promotional strategies, messages and performance,
- Distribution and pricing
- Sales Volume/Units—Historical, one-year goal, long-term goals
- Growth/Loss—share trends and possible reasons
- Features—strengths, weaknesses, differentiators
- Brand Image/Position/Perceptions/Culture
- Advertising Budget

Competition
- Who—list major competitors
- Sales/Share—units, price (purchase/lease), % volume, key segments, trends
- Target markets
- Growth/loss/decline and reasons
- Advertising/promotions budget
- Advertising share of voice
- Positioning, messaging, and promotions
- Distribution channels
- Overall brand and product strengths/weaknesses
- Identify (as needed)
  - Leader
  - Up-and-comer
  - In trouble
  - Basic positioning, strategy, strengths and weaknesses

Category
- Category history
- Size—sales and unit volume
- Growth/Loss—trends and reasons
- Penetration of usage/purchase
- Key distributional channels
- Geography
- Seasonality
- SWOT (see next section)
- Major disruptions facing category

Consumer/Customer
- Major use/role of product
- Demographics (gender, age, income, family status, geography, emerging markets)
- Key segments (types/sizes, shifts/growth, spending, opportunities)
- Consumer perceptions of brand/product
- Psychographic measures like attitudes, beliefs, opinions, and values
- Lifestyle activities, hobbies, affinities
- Life stage (e.g., new parent, first-time homeowner, retirement)
- Influencers/advocates/ambassadors
- Shopping and decision-making behaviors
- Product usage habits and behaviors
- Purchase funnel
- Cultural trends
- Media consumption (channel, use, time spent)

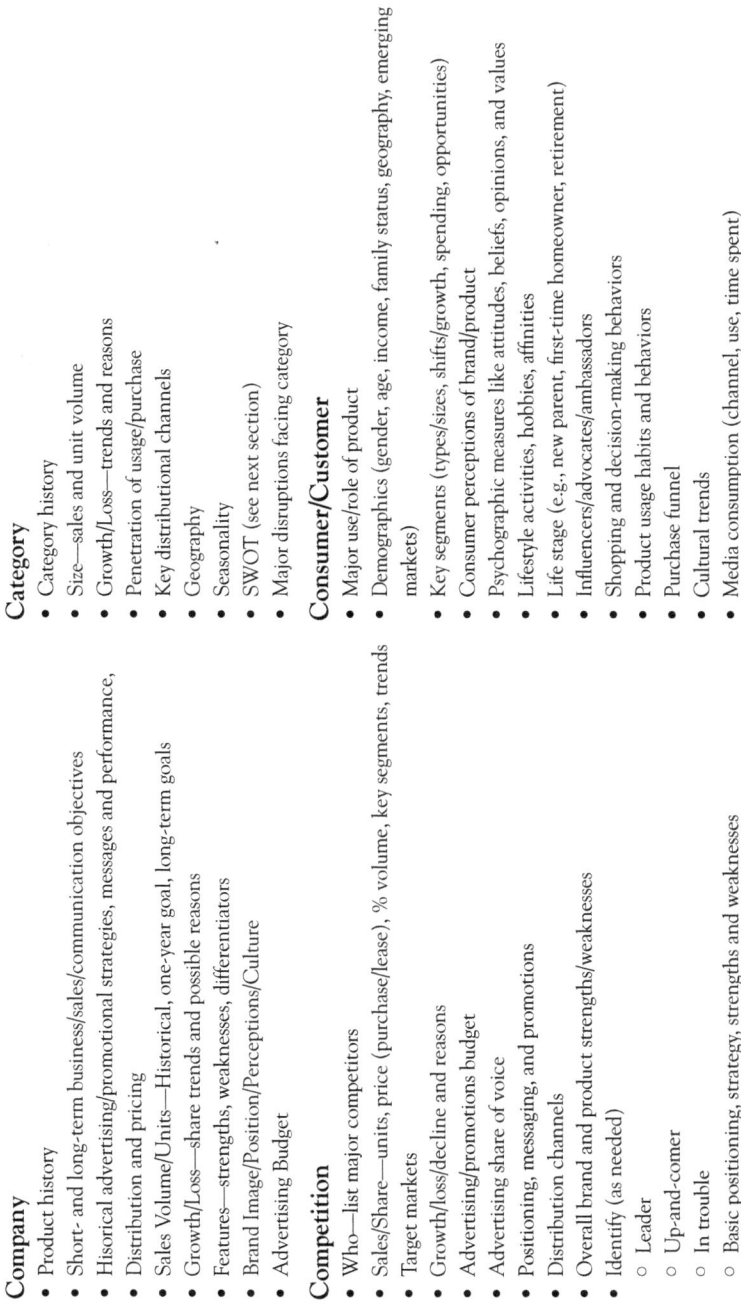

Figure 3.7 The 4Cs

	Internal (controllable)	External (uncontrollable)
Leverage + Build	**Strengths** Build on internal strengths	**Opportunities** Leverage external opportunities
Manage + Overcome	**Weaknesses** Address internal weaknesses	**Threats** Address and avoid external threats

Figure 3.8 SWOT Analysis

Additionally, as SMEs look to enter new markets, it is helpful to conduct a supplemental PESTLE analysis (introduced in Part One) that looks specifically at the new market's **p**olitical, **e**conomic, **s**ocial, techni-cal, **l**egal, and **e**nvironmental factors that may influence future business and marketing decisions. The following list identifies additional key ques-tions that SMEs will want to explore and address when evaluating the U.S. market entry opportunity:

- Are there laws, legislation, or regulatory agencies and/or manufac-turing considerations that affect your business? If so, how?
- How sensitive is your business to economic factors like inflation, recession, and cost of living?
- Are there any manufacturing or distribution advantages or disad-vantages versus the competition's?
- Are there technological trends that may be affecting your business? New technologies? Waning or declining technologies?
- What is the demographic nature of the new market? How is it changing?
- What are the cultural and personal values of your buyer and end-user market? Are they effectively being addressed by your company? Are they changing? How?
- Are there any untapped potential buyers/users that should be con-sidered? If so, who? Why?
- Are there any unmet needs/wants in the market that you can fulfill?
- What are the strongest features/attributes of your product/service versus the competition's? Which are the weakest?
- Are there any patents or IP that you need to be aware of?
- How is your competitor's product different (or better)?

- Is your product offering easy or difficult to change, update, or innovate? How might this affect your market entry strategy?
- Where does your pricing stand versus the competition's? Are your margins sufficient?
- Do your prices fluctuate (due to competition, seasonality, sales, or discounts) or do they remain stable? Is your pricing vulnerable to shifts in foreign currency?
- What communication elements are currently being employed? What is working? What isn't? Why?
- What are the predominant perceptions in the marketplace about your product or service? Are they positive, negative, or neutral?
- Where is the product or service currently sold? What is working? What isn't?
- Are there any marketing channels (e.g., distribution) that aren't currently being exploited and that could and should be? Similarly, are there channels that struggle or are waning in popularity?
- What barriers stand in the way of purchase?
- Is your brand known? Are consumers aware of it? What are their perceptions?

Market Research Methods

There are two basic approaches to conducting market research: (1) quantitative and (2) qualitative research. Quantitative is referred to as data that defines whereas qualitative is data that describes. Both approaches come with their unique advantages and drawbacks. On the one hand, quantitative research (e.g., market or product surveys) enables firms to generate objective, quantifiable findings that allow comparisons and statistical analysis. The drawback to quantitative research (as we saw with the case of the New Coke introduction) is that it fails to account for emotions and nuances in consumer responses. On the other hand, conducting qualitative research enables firms to explore research issues and questions in greater depth, including the ability to elicit emotional responses and the *why* behind responses. Needless to say, an important limitation of qualitative research is that it is not projectable to larger audiences, as a handful of interviews or focus groups are not a statistically reliable sample size.

Quantitative Survey Tools

Given that surveys remain the most used quantitative research tool, we'll focus on the survey method in this section. Four leading self-service survey platforms include Survey Monkey (surveymonkey.com), Toluna Quick Surveys (quicksurveys.com), Google Surveys (surveys.google.com), and Qualtrics (qualtrics.com). All four offer great features for survey design (including mobile optimization), deployment, analysis, and reporting as well as customizable respondent sampling. Customizable sampling can be very helpful when you don't have a database of names, which is often the case when seeking to understand and enter new markets. As with most categories, these platforms each have unique advantages and disadvantages. We recommend that you spend time getting to know and understanding each platform's benefits and limitations when it comes to sample sourcing, features, and functionality before beginning your research.

As a quantitative research approach, surveys can be particularly valuable when assessing the influence of your branding strategy on sales or other key success indicators. It's common for companies to use longitudinal surveys (e.g., annual or biannual) for brand assessment studies, where your brand's performance is tracked over time. Surveys can also be useful for tracking brand awareness and customer attitudes with respect to specific areas such as product and service offerings and customer service efforts. Finally, numerous firms use online surveys to generate new ideas for product offerings.

A common starting place for SMEs looking to enter a new market is to conduct an awareness, attitude, and usage (AA&U) study that seeks to understand awareness, perceptions, knowledge, and use behavior for your company versus key competitor brands. This can be periodically updated to understand where ground has been gained or lost over time, and it is especially helpful when executed with marketing efforts like advertising and product launches. There are two key types of awareness—aided and unaided—that the marketer may be interested in measuring. Aided awareness simply means that the research respondent has heard of a brand name, usually contained within a list of competitors; it is called aided awareness because the respondent's memory is aided by the list. An aided awareness question might include something like, "Which of the following list of energy drinks have you heard of?" Unaided awareness, on the other hand, measures what marketers call *top-of-mind* awareness, a highly coveted space in the consumer's mind. Without any mention of the brand (an especially important question for survey design), an unaided awareness question might go something like, "List the first three energy drinks that come to mind."

For instance, an SME entering the U.S. market could create a brand awareness survey using Qualtrics or SurveyMonkey to assess how familiar consumers are with a new brand and to track awareness and familiarity levels over time. Similarly, depending on the extent of your market presence, you could extend your brand awareness to study brand usage and attributes (e.g., purchase frequency, competitor purchases, product usage and feedback) as well as current and future purchase intent.

Given that reliable and projectable quantitative research can often be costly and time consuming, many marketers consider omnibus studies or purchase syndicated research. Omnibus studies are essentially collective studies where multiple marketers come together to conduct one study, each submitting select custom questions to be distributed to a wide sample of respondents. This approach allows for greater scale and lower costs. Similarly, companies like Simmons, MRI, IRI, and Nielsen offer what is called syndicated data. Simmons (www.simmonsresearch .com/), for example, surveys over 25,000 U.S. adult respondents and collects responses on over 500 product categories, 8,000 brands, 600 attitudes and psychographic measures, and thousands of media properties. In addition, Simmons conducts a variety of segmentation and supplemental studies like its Hispanic, Teen, and Local Market studies. Other research companies like IRI and Nielsen collect and sell sophisticated large data sets on topics such as consumer packaged goods pricing and purchase behavior, media consumption, and more.

Qualitative Techniques

There are numerous qualitative research techniques available to companies. These techniques include in-depth one-on-one interviews (IDI), focus groups, and observational research. Three important considerations when determining qualitative research approaches include (1) how much time do you want to spend with each respondent, (2) how many respondents would you like to speak to, and (3) how much control would you like to exert over your research approach? A typical focus group lasts 2 hours and contains 8 to 10 respondents; this means that each person gets 12 to 15 minutes of time to speak. Conversely, a typical IDI lasts about an hour, giving you 60 minutes with that one individual. Observational research enables researchers to observe more *natural* consumer behavior with lessened response bias. Therefore, each approach has its pros and cons. It's important to note that there are typically costs associated with *recruiting* respondents for focus groups and IDIs. This is in addition to the *incentives* paid to motivate the respondent to show up and pay full attention during the entire session; incentives typically begin at $75 per person and go higher depending on whom you are talking to. For example, doctors tend to cost more than college students. A less expensive approach is with what is called *woman- and man-on-the-street* research, where the researcher approaches potential respondents and offers a small incentive, often a gift card, for their involvement. This approach, however, obviously doesn't allow the research as much control or time with the respondent.

For the aforementioned reasons, when entering new markets, access to individuals or groups of individuals within a specific market with traditional qualitative research methods may be difficult, too costly, or too time consuming. Fortunately, there are some cost-effective and powerful social listening tools that allow you to essentially *eavesdrop on the Internet.* Imagine being able to put a cup to the Internet's window and not only listen in on the billions of thoughts and conversations that people are sharing about products and brands, but to also use the tool to search for the volume and sentiment (positive or negative) of the specific conversations that are happening regarding specific product categories and brands. Imagine also being able to quickly quantify, understand, and compare these conversations within or across markets. And imagine you had a real-time, online listening device that gave you deep insight into people's failures, frustrations, families, work life, products, habits, preferences, wishes, wants, needs, losses, and desires. This is all possible via a variety of online and social media listening platforms that have emerged over the past several years. Some of the leading platforms include Crimson Hexagon, Sysomos, Radian6, and NetBase. These platforms typically charge monthly service fees in order for users to get full access to the billions (trillions in some cases) of data points and powerful processing tools. There are also a variety of free platforms such as Social Mention, HowSociable, Facebook Insights, Twitter Analytics, and Google Trends. While the free versions clearly have their limitations, when used effectively, each can offer the new market entrant a plethora of useful information. Finally, don't underestimate the power of user reviews. Analyzing reviews on sites like Yelp and Amazon can yield incredible insights into consumer wants and needs as well as competitive weaknesses.

There are a number of other free and highly informative resources worth mentioning from which the foreign SME can gain valuable insights into the U.S. consumer and marketplace:

- *U.S. Demographics*: The government census website (www.census .gov) contains historical U.S. demographic census data like population size, ethnicity, occupation, income, and more.
- *Public Opinion*: PEW Research Center (www.pewresearch.com) is the preeminent nonpartisan research center that measures public opinion and behaviors around politics, technology, social trends, religion, and more.
- *Consumer and Cultural Trends*: For cutting-edge trends on fashion, tech, design, culture, communications, and marketing check out Trendhunter (www.trendhunter.com), PSFK (www.psfk.com), and JWT Intelligence (www.jwtintelligence.com).
- *Industry News and Competitive Insights*: For the latest industry and tech trends sign up for newsletters like Smartbrief (www.smartbrief .com), eMarketer (www.emarketer.com), and Media Post (www .mediapost.com).

The Power of an Insight

With respect to generating market research, there's an important distinction to be made between merely *collecting information* and *generating true insights*. Information is just that—raw numbers or statistics or text that on its own doesn't really reveal much beyond the content. An insight, though, represents a higher level meaning behind the observation. This is what we call *the story behind the data*. For example, an observation in the pet food industry could be that more and more pet owners are spending more and more money on healthy, organic food for their pets. Ok, that's interesting. But what is *even more* interesting could be the insight behind that observation—that for some pet owners, their precious dogs or cats are as important as their children, and are treated as such. Or, that we as humans often feel a seemingly irrational need to pamper our pets, in part because they are totally dependent on us.

Observations that lead to the development of insights can lead to shifts in brand positioning, allow the marketer to see and respond to market or product changes before anyone else, and sometimes even enable a company to change an entire industry. For example, Apple's original insights with respect to computers and computing were driven by the insight that there was an emotional element of design and aesthetics that drove people to buy its products. Instead of simply producing and selling boxes containing hardware and software, Apple created beautifully designed computers, laptops, mobile devices, and smartphones that happened to function as good or better than its competitors'. In this way, insights can be and should be applied to the development of targeting strategy, product development, packaging, distribution methods, and brand planning and messaging.

However, getting from observation to insight seldom involves a straight line and is never simple. It involves the messy process of exploration, reading, comparing, pulling apart, walking away, getting confused, taking notes, re-reading notes, and maybe even taking a short walk with your dog. It involves digging deep for the higher-level meanings inherent in your observations and your data. The more data points, especially interesting ones, that you have, the greater the likelihood that you will strike gold by uncovering an insight.

An incredibly simple, yet extremely effective, tip to uncovering deep insights is to keep asking "Why?" The closer you get to the psychology behind a consumer's decision, the most likely you are to get to a truly deep insight.

How Dos Equis Became the Most Interesting Beer in the World

Prior to its 2006 U.S. launch, Dos Equis was merely an unfamiliar Mexican beer brand competing in the shadow of the leading U.S. Mexican beer import, Corona. In order to survive, let alone succeed, in the struggling yet highly competitive import category, the team in charge of developing and growing the Dos Equis brand in the United States knew it needed to push it into a space (what we call a *whitespace*) that was not only different from that of any other competing beer but was also relevant and meaningful to the core young 18 to 34 year-old male consumer. On the one hand, Corona, the number #1 Mexican import, had dominated the Mexican beer category with visions of tranquil, white sand beaches and endless summers. Domestic American beers, on the other hand, existed in the realm of scantily clad women, sports, and sophomoric guy humor. Further, the craft beer segment, one of the only beer segments seeing growth, stood for craftsmanship and quality.

The research and planning team working on growing the Dos Equis brand in the U.S. market began their search for brand meaning and market differentiation with consumer research, but not your typical market research that relied upon surveys or focus groups. They knew that in order to identify a truly powerful insight about their core young male target they needed do something different—so they actually went to the bar and drank with them. (Not a bad job for an up-and-coming market researcher!) One of the things that they *observed* was that guys like to tell *tall tales*—stories that exaggerate, embellish, and sometimes present outright fabrications about their lives and experiences. The 20-cm fish they actually caught suddenly grows to become a meter long and the 5-km hike in a local forest becomes a 20-km trek through the Australian Outback. Interested in this phenomenon, the researchers asked these guys the questions of "Why, why, and why" again and again, and eventually learned that one of a guy's biggest fears in life is to be seen as boring among his peers and just like every other guy! This idea eventually led to the consumer insight of "I'd rather be dead than boring," which eventually gave birth to the *Most Interesting Man in the World* campaign—an embodiment of the Dos Equis brand and a fictitious, relatively older spokesperson described as "a man rich in stories and experiences, much the way the audience hopes to be in the future." Following is the tongue-in-cheek radio script that helped to launch the brand:

With a backdrop of dramatic music, an announcer voice says,

It's been said he buried a time capsule full of things that haven't happened yet. His bear hugs are actually hugs he gives to bears.

If he disagrees with you, it's because you were wrong.
He is . . . The Most Interesting Man in the World

The raspy and wise voice of a man with a Spanish accent ends the
spot with,

I don't always drink beer, but when I do, I prefer Dos Equis.
Stay thirsty my friends.

The campaign not only became a pop-culture phenomenon, but more
importantly, it helped grow sales. Dos Equis' U.S. sales increased each
year between 2006 and 2010 and tripled in Canada in 2008. Market data
indicate that North American sales of Dos Equis increased by 22 percent
at a time when other imported beers fell by 4 percent. How's that for an
insight? From this example and others, it is clear that many of the world's
most transformative marketing efforts are firmly rooted in market research
and observations that have led to the development of deep, meaningful,
and inspiring consumer insights.

Identifying Your Market: Segmentation and Targeting

The concepts of market segmentation and targeting are central to helping
formulate and guide your research plan and executing a successful market entry strategy. *Market segmentation* involves the process of identifying
subgroups of people or organizations that share certain meaningful characteristics and possess distinct needs and wants. The concept of market
segmentation, therefore, is as applicable to business-to-business (B2B) as
it is to business-to-consumer (B2C) markets. One easy way to describe it
is that the opposite of market segmentation is mass marketing, or offering
one product or advertising campaign to all consumers. Although this is
most often the most efficient approach—one product or one campaign
for the masses—it is obvious that such an approach is neither realistic nor
effective given what we know about the diversity of the U.S. consumer
market. It shouldn't come as a surprise that not all buyers are the same.
Different groups have different purchase reasons and motives.

One revealing market segmentation example is how the Germany-based
athletic shoe brand Adidas has grown its business in the United States.
In the 1960s and 70s, athletic shoes were sold primarily to those who

engaged in some type of sport. Fast forward to the 2000s, and the athletic footwear market is segmented in many ways, including sports-specific consumers (e.g., tennis or basketball players or runners), athleisure (wearing athletic shoes for leisure activities such as hanging out with friends), and for fashion. For the nonsports segment, Adidas has its Originals line of shoes, Reebok has what it calls its Classics category, and Puma has even developed a market segment for its shoes on the basis of young consumers' usage when going out to bars at night. Although you may not see these types of shoes on the medal stand at the next Olympics, you can be sure that the sales volume for these nonsports segments dwarfs that of sales to sports-specific usage.

In terms of segmentation approaches, there are many ways to divide and segment a market. For instance, beverage brands such as Gatorade, Coca-Cola, or Pepsi and entertainment companies such as Disney develop segmentation strategies on the basis of *demographic* factors such as age or *psychographic* factors such as personality, self-perception, and behavioral patterns. Often, segmentation strategies will align with or lead to the development of related product category segments. For example, the sizable beverage market in the United States is defined by numerous category segments such as carbonated soft drinks, fruit beverages, bottled waters, sports drinks, and caffeinated drinks. Demographic market segmentation variables can include gender (e.g., Gillette develops specific shaving products for males and females), income and social class (e.g., Walmart appeals to lower-income and Barney's to higher-income shoppers), and ethnicity (e.g., Modelo's growth among the Hispanic American population in the beer category). Psychographic segmentation variables might include consumers' interests, attitudes, and opinions. Another form of segmentation, involving digital advertising, is called *geotargeting*, where consumers in certain local markets are shown specific advertisements (e.g., banner ads or online video content) based on characteristics of those markets. One market segmentation database that combines psychographic factors such as lifestyles with geography and socioeconomic data is PRIZM, which slices the U.S. market into 66 different segments, some of which are called the Shotguns and Pickups, Rural Industrial, and Starter Families segments. And, these 66 PRIZM segments are available for use in the Simmons syndicated data set mentioned previously.

When deciding what market segments to pursue, it is important to choose segments that meet four important segmentation criteria:

1. Is the segment identifiable and measurable in terms of size of market opportunity?
2. Is it substantial enough and unique to other segments in order to afford the cost and effort of developing a unique marketing mix for the segment(s)?
3. Is it accessible in terms of being able to reach and communicate with consumers within the segment?
4. Will consumers within the segment respond favorably to your marketing mix offerings?

Developing a targeting strategy involves developing your marketing mix (including product, pricing, place/distribution, and advertising/promotions) for specific target market segments. The trade-offs related to the development of targeting strategies revolve around the question, "How many segments should you identify?" In other words, the question is whether a company should choose one large target audience or multiple smaller ones. On the one hand, an *undifferentiated targeting strategy* is one that includes a large population of consumers. The benefit of this approach is that it can be more efficient for a company to develop a standardized marketing mix of products, pricing, and advertising, as well as distribution outlets, to reach a large number of customers. The risk is that it assumes that a single product or service and one brand or marketing communications message will sufficiently appeal to that large group of consumers. In the United States, Walmart or Costco are examples of retailers following an undifferentiated targeting strategy. On the other hand, a *differentiated targeting strategy* is one where the company develops multiple products (along with related communications and campaigns) for different consumer segments, or targets. This approach enables companies to appeal more directly to customer needs or wants with distinct marketing mixes developed for multiple targets. For example, Toyota represents an automotive company with sub-brands of cars (Toyota, Lexus, Prius) that appeal to many types of car buyers' demographic and psychographic characteristics. The one drawback to such a targeting strategy is that it is more complex and expensive and involves greater company resources.

Leveraging segmentation and seeking to identify untapped consumer needs and wants are both solid strategies for gaining relevance with your target(s). Thinking back to Dos Equis, the broad market segment was young men (because they drink the majority of the beer!) but the specific target was young men who want to feel interesting. Target market identification and selection are part science and part art, and there aren't many free tools (that we know of) to help marketers identify their audience(s). That said, consider utilizing Facebook's free Audience Insights tool (www .facebook.com/ads/audience-insights) to explore, understand, and size audiences using a variety of demographics such as age, income, and geography as well as specific interests, affinities, and behaviors such ice hockey, yoga, and fashion.

For example, Facebook estimates that there are 800,000 to 900,000 women 18 to 34 years old in the United States who are interested in Peru. Figure 3.9 illustrates other examples of insights you can glean from the Audience Insights. It's worth noting, however, that at the time of writing this book, Facebook has also been under scrutiny for inaccurate numbers cited within its resources. As with all research, it is meant to inform and guide *and not* represent the ultimate decision criteria.

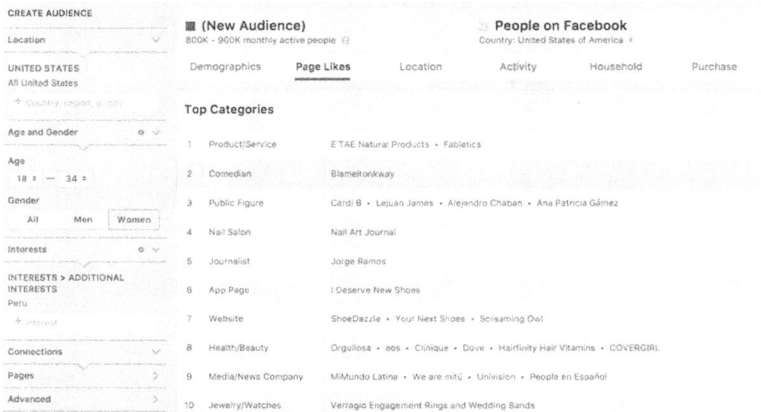

Figure 3.9 Screengrab from Facebook audience insights tool

Questions to Consider

- What key opportunities, challenges, and action items emerged from your 4Cs, PESTLE, and SWOT analyses?
- What further research do you need to conduct? What type of research approach—qualitative, quantitative, social listening, or a combination thereof—might best suit your needs?
- What are the most important market segmentation variables that you might want to consider? How many segments emerge and how large are they? What are the pros and cons of each?

CHAPTER 4

Building and Activating Your Brand

I would like to be remembered, if I am remembered at all, as being a catalyst for change in the world, change for good.
—Rupert Murdoch (1931–present), Australian-born American media mogul.

Main points in this chapter
- Building and positioning a powerful and purpose-driven brand
- From planning to execution: developing the marketing mix
- Marketing analytics: measure, test, learn, optimize

Building and Positioning a Powerful and Purpose-Driven Brand

As we've discussed thus far, successful market entry strategies are based on numerous factors, including existing market size, competition, and the comparable strengths and uniqueness of the market entrant's product or service offering. Moreover, for many SMEs, consumers' first exposure to, and lasting impression of, your company relates to what we refer to as the *brand*. Numerous studies have shown that the advantages to, and benefits of, a powerful brand in a crowded market like the United States include building increased market awareness and purchase intent as well as customer trust, confidence, and loyalty. Because of this, developing your brand (including brand strategy, brand meaning, and brand purpose) might be the single most important step for an SME entering the highly competitive U.S. market.

When discussing brand strategy, we often first ask our students the seemingly simple question: What is a brand? Their answers often equate a brand with a two-dimensional visual representation of the company, what we call a *logo,* and a name. However, your brand and brand strategy go far beyond crafting a logo and catchy name like Google, Apple or Nike. Your brand and what it represents to consumers is ultimately defined through the careful expression of what we call the *4Ps* of marketing: product, price, place (e.g., distribution, retail outlets), and promotion. The American Marketing Association defines a brand as "A name, term, design, symbol or any other feature that identifies one seller's good or service as distinct from those of other sellers." While this is certainly an accurate definition, we think it fails to capture some of the most powerful elements of what a properly engineered brand contains. Sergio Zyman, former Coca-Cola Company chief marketing officer, argues that a brand is "the bundle of functional and emotional benefits, attributes, icons and symbols that, in total, comprise the meaning of the product or service." Scott Bedbury, the former Nike and Starbucks marketing executive, calls a brand simply "the idea of the thing."

Whichever way we define the concept of a brand, we can agree that it represents the meaning and purpose attached to a company and is a critical element of any SME's strategy to enter the U.S. market. Brands represent, and are communicated by, everything associated with the company, including its employees, products and services, advertising, stores or website, social media presence, packaging, pricing, country of origin, and yes, visual look (e.g., through its logo and brand-defining color and design). Considering the world's great brands (Apple, Google, BMW, Nike, Starbucks, and more), they all have built into their brand strategy continuity across customer touchpoints, including consistency of logo, color, design, tone, message, and purpose.

In this chapter, we propose that the three most important *branding* steps (as shown in Figure 4.1) to consider when entering the U.S. market are to (1) identify your target market, the customers you *must* reach in order to be successful, including their wants and needs; (2) make sure your product offering is aligned with your target consumer; and (3) given your target market and product offering, effectively position your brand against your competition. The central idea with your brand strategy is to

Target market

Your product   Competitive positioning

Figure 4.1 The marketing triangle

identify the white space in terms of your target market, product or service offering, and competitive positioning. The key question you should ask related to your brand strategy is, What can you do differently or better than your competition and, in doing so, identify any unaddressed targets, needs, wants, and unique messaging?

Branding expert Kevin Lane Keller argues, "Building and properly managing brand equity has become a priority for companies of all sizes, in all types of industries, in all types of markets."[1] In his brand research, Keller has identified the most common traits that the world's strongest brands share. These traits include excelling at delivering benefits that your customers' desire, remaining relevant amidst changes in technology and consumer behavior, and being strategically positioned vis-à-vis your *competition* as well as leveraging your *unique points of difference.*

Target Audience

As discussed in Chapter 3, decisions regarding the size and composition of your target audience have profound implications on brand and product development, communications, pricing, and distribution. When defining your brand (and everything it stands for), defining your target audience is a critical first step. The sheer size of the United States in terms of population, market size, and spending power is certainly appealing. How difficult can it be to enter a market with 330 million people? As we argued previously, it can be and is *very* difficult. Why? You're most

---

[1]K. L. Keller. January–February 2000. "The Brand Report Card," *Harvard Business Review.*

likely not the first company—the first mover, the pioneer brand—in your respective market. In fact, you're most likely competing against hundreds if not thousands of entrenched companies. This means that you face significant competition, and lots of it. Moreover, when defining your target audience, identifying a larger audience is not necessarily an advantage. Imagine you're looking to enter the U.S. market with a new sports drink. You may view your target audience as all males and females between the age of 25 and 45 who play sports or engage in some type of fitness activity more than once per week. You've defined a market size that is a subset of approximately 125 million prospective customers. But don't forget—you're also competing against several large and entrenched brands, including Gatorade and Powerade, fueled by massive parent companies with seemingly unlimited budgets.

The key to target audience definition is to begin with a relatively wide demographic profile (e.g., males and females between the age of 25 and 45 who play sports or engage in some fitness activity at least once per week) and move to a narrower profile based on psychographics (e.g., what they think, feel, identify with, are motivated by). Perhaps your product makeup is one that is organic or developed in Japan with the country's best sports medicine and physiologists. Thus, your product offering may give you license to appeal to a more aspirational athlete or fitness buff who really cares what they put into their bodies. This, in turn, narrows your target market from who you *could sell to* (the 125 million males and females in the United States) to who you *would like to sell to* (a subset of these 125 million individuals) to who you *really need to sell to* in order to be successful (a more narrowly defined target audience of perhaps the 125 million people in the United States who are avid sports and fitness enthusiasts).

Product

The next step in building and positioning a successful brand involves your product or service offering. Without a strong product or service offering, one that fills a distinct consumer need or want, all the branding in the world won't help. Strong products are those that fill a need and ultimately add, or are perceived as delivering, value in the consumer's mind.

The challenge marketers face, particularly those seeking to enter the U.S. market, involves product proliferation. In most, if not all industries, particularly consumer goods industries, there is a surfeit, a glut, of products available. This is what author Scott Bedbury, in his book *A New Brand World*, refers to as *commodity-like products*: products sold by brands that are functionally no different from their competitors' products. For instance, Apple's portfolio of iPhones is (for the most part) similar to Samsung's smartphone devices where the latest iPhone possesses some unique advantages, so does the new Samsung Galaxy. Some of what differentiates these two products lies within the definition of a product (e.g., design, style, functionality), yet much of what sets these two smartphones apart relates to how the brand is perceived by consumers. The Apple brand is known as innovative, stylish, the smartphone pioneer, prestigious even, where Samsung has struggled with how it is perceived by consumers as a *me-too* brand trying to compete against Apple. One can apply the same thought process to the automotive industry where a car made by BMW is viewed as superior to the offerings of other car brands not only because of how its cars are designed and produced, and how they perform, but also how the brand is viewed by car consumers as unique.

Thus, designing, producing, and bringing to market a quality product is no longer enough in today's hypercompetitive U.S. marketplace. So, in addition to identifying your target audience and offering that fills needs and wants, perhaps the #1 success factor for many products is how well they are positioned in a crowded marketplace filled with commodity-like competing offerings.

Competitive Positioning

At its core, marketing is about value creation (real or perceived) and differentiation (buy this, not that). One of the most powerful marketing tools is something called *positioning*. In its simplest terms, positioning is simply the space (the position) that the brand owns and occupies in its consumers' mind. For example, the leading pain-reliever brand Advil has spent decades and hundreds of millions of dollars to claim and maintain the top-of-mind association with *relieves all types of pain* among U.S. consumers (Figure 4.2).

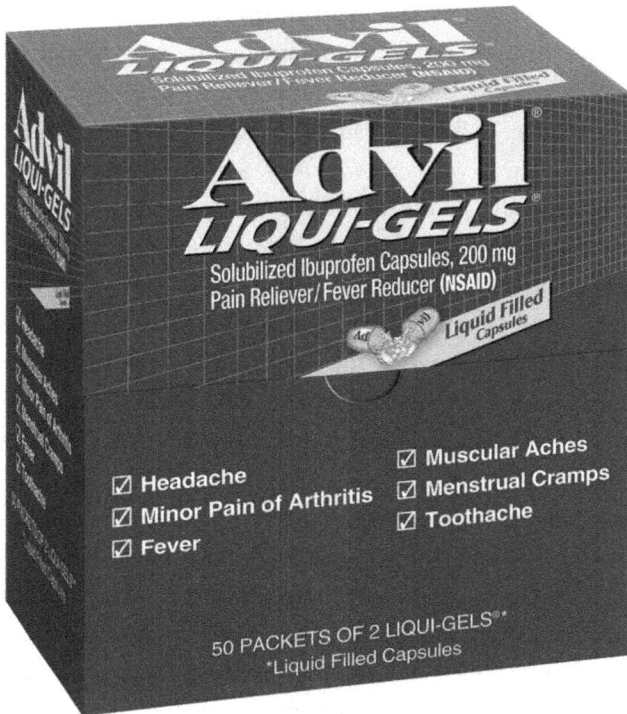

Figure 4.2 Advil counter top box

Over time, Advil came to *own* the all-around pain reliever space in the consumer's mind. When people have some sort of ache or pain, the first thing to come to mind for most is Advil. This immediate association equates to billions of dollars in sales. Meanwhile, Excedrin, another pain reliever, needed to position itself in a competitive position and chose to claim the differentiated and necessary association with *headaches* (Figure 4.3). Excedrin quickly became the default choice specifically for headache relief.

A simple, yet powerful, exercise for any product wishing stand out and stand for something (a solid goal for any business wishing to build a brand) is to craft a positioning statement. The classic positioning statement answers four questions: (1) Who are you for? (2) What is your promise/What makes you different and/or better? (3) What is the proof to support your claim? (4) In what category do you play (this determines your competitive set, which is necessary for differentiation)?

Figure 4.3 Excedrin digital ad unit

Turned into a sentence, a positioning statement becomes "For (target), (brand) offers (promise) in (category). Unlike (competition), (brand) offers (reasons to believe)."

For example, Advil's positioning statement might be something like, "For people who don't have time for downtime, Advil offers the fastest and most effective pain relief. Multiple clinical trials have shown that ibuprofen in Advil is stronger and lasts longer than the active ingredients in both Tylenol and Excedrin."

Competitive positioning isn't only about defining your product's functional offering (including benefits, quality, and performance); it can also help you carve out other ways to differentiate your offering in the mind of the consumer. How you position your brand, then, becomes the foundation for your marketing strategy and message. Consider the following brands and their competitive positioning strategies:

- Out-positioning the competition: 7-up "The Uncola," Avis rental cars "We're #2 we try harder"

- A strict focus on a relevant and understandable benefit (consumer need): Crest Toothpaste equals reduced cavities
- Consistent attributes that transcend the 4Ps: Hilton Garden Inns translate to economical comfort whereas Four Seasons hotels convey luxury in every imaginable sense
- Usage occasion: the Jeep Wrangler as an urban off-road vehicle
- Brand Purpose: TOMS and its One-for-One Giving Program that defines its business model

A recent example of brilliant brand positioning and market-entry prowess involves a serendipitous meeting at a party between a first-time entrepreneur and a guy who knew someone with thousands of razor blades collecting dust in a warehouse. The first-time entrepreneur, Michael Dubin, came up with a unique way to find a market for all these blades. (Remember, it's difficult to imagine a product more commodity-like than simple razor blades.) The idea was not to simply try to resell the blades as excess inventory to a big player in the men's hygiene market. The bigger idea, one that led to the brilliant brand positioning strategy, was to develop a monthly subscription-based razor delivery service called the Dollar Shave Club where men could get their razors and blades delivered straight to their bathroom door, enabling them to avoid the tedious process of trying to buy overpriced razors and blades at retail.

Dollar Shave Club's competitive positioning strategy was to disrupt the behemoth men's shaving industry and its age-old conventions: man enters store, tries in vain to locate a store associate to unlock the precious razors and blades cabinet, waits for them to unlock it, and overpays for said razors and blades. Another convention that Dubin disrupted was the traditional way that brands communicated their positioning. Traditionally, to launch a new venture in the billion-plus dollar men's hygiene market would take millions of dollars in commercial production and media spending. In 2012, Dubin produced the now-famous launch video, as shown in Figure 4.4, for less than $5,000 and distributed it for free on YouTube. Within days, the homegrown video had gone viral and more recently approached 25 million YouTube views. Not a bad return on a $4,500 investment. Further, almost five years after the company was

Figure 4.4 Screengrab from Dollar Shave Club YouTube launch video, 2012

founded, it was bought by Unilever for $1 billion. Dollar Shave Club's positioning points to *a better way to shave* and is nicely encapsulated in their tagline, "Shave Time, Shave Money." *Source*: http://www.nytimes.com/2013/04/11/business/smallbusiness/dollar-shave-club-from-viral-video-to-real-business.html

In sum, looking at its brand positioning strategy, Dollar Shave Club identified and successfully disrupted these long-held category conventions, the combination of which led to its meteoric rise:

Category convention	Disruption
Razor blades are expensive, so much so that people use them until they are dull and ineffective.	Dollar Shave Club makes them cheap and good; that way you can use a fresh blade when you need to.
The purchase process for razor blades is cumbersome and inefficient. They are merchandised and sold as if they were the Crown Jewels, located behind locked cases in the store.	Dollar Shave Club conveniently sends them right to your home.
Razor blade advertising lacks personality, and all brands apply the same template—ads that feature perfect-looking celebrities and models who don't even grow facial hair.	Dollar Shave Club commercials feature its founder, Michael Dubin, and tells it like it is with a sassy, irreverent, and humorous tone. Dollar Shave Club's irreverent brand personality is consistent and pervasive on the website, packaging, in-package newsletters, e-mails, and other collateral materials.

Another well-executed brand positioning example in the shaving space involves the Dutch brand Phillips and its ShaveEverywhere campaign. Back in 2006, Phillips wanted to grow its share of the men's grooming market in the United States. At the time, the concept of the metrosexual male (males who cared about the appearance of their skin and hair, for example) was taking hold in the United States, evidenced by increased sales of men's skin care and hair care products. In response, Phillips created a dynamic website—shaveeverywhere.com—that portrayed in subtle and humorous terms the benefits of shaving those *intimate* areas. A central element of Phillips' new campaign was to limit traditional media and maximize its web exposure. In the end, shaveeverywhere.com attracted millions of visitors and video views while seamlessly communicating the benefits of Phillips electric shavers in a way that engaged young males.[2] Through this competitive brand positioning, Phillips was able to establish an even greater foothold in the U.S. shaving market.

Purpose-Driven Positioning

One modern twist on brand positioning relates to how more and more brands are defining themselves as purpose driven and mission based. William Clay Ford, Jr., former board chairman and CEO of Ford Motor Company remarked, "A good company offers excellent products and services. A great company also offers excellent products and services, but also strives to make the world a better place." What this means is that beyond producing a quality product, brands increasingly are seeking to differentiate themselves through a well-defined higher-level purpose or mission. For example, the TOMS brand sells casual shoes, sunglasses, and other accessory items on the basis of its One-for-One model, whereby for each product sale, TOMS works with countries in developing markets such as Africa to distribute related products (such as shoes) to people in need.

Similar to the TOMS model, at the corporate level, global multibrand companies such as Unilever have begun to take notice of the

---

[2]http://adage.com/article/digital/philips-brave-shave-campaign/131162/

effects of purpose-driven brand strategies on the bottom line (i.e., sales and brand growth).[3] As a first step toward purpose-based positioning of its brands, Unilever commissioned research to examine what factors seemed to influence individuals' purchase behavior, with an eye on household products. What it found was that a majority of consumers consider the concept of *environmental sustainability* important when buying products such as cleaning products and food items. In response, Unilever grouped a family of its most progressive brands in terms of sustainability practices, brands such as Lifebuoy, Ben & Jerry's, and Dove, in what it called its "Sustainable Living" brands. According to *Marketing Week*, these are among the Unilever brands that are leading the company in terms of sustainability and social purpose. In terms of brand performance, these brands are also growing faster than the remainder of Unilever brands.

To put the movement toward purpose-driven brands in perspective, it is helpful to first look back at recent history. The recent financial markets meltdown of 2007 through 2009, what some refer to as the "great recession," significantly changed the American consumer psyche. Prior to the recession, many Americans had strong confidence in American business, belief that the U.S. economy was on firm ground, and to some degree faith that the U.S. government would protect them from danger and misfortune. When markets began to crash in December 2007, resulting in millions of jobs, retirement funds, and pensions lost, Americans felt abandoned or betrayed. According to the PEW Research Center,[4] trust in government had been on a steady decline since 2001, reaching an all-time low in 2011 where only one in five Americans reported "trusting the government in Washington all or some of the time." Moreover, the 2009 Edelman Trust Barometer Survey[5] indicated that 77 percent of Americans say that they trust corporations less now than they did a year ago, and in a 2010 study Edelman[6] reported that 87 percent of global

---

[3]https://www.marketingweek.com/2017/05/18/unilever-sustainable-brands-growth/

[4]http://www.people-press.org/2017/05/03/public-trust-in-government-1958-2017/

[5]https://www.edelman.com/assets/uploads/2014/01/2009-Trust-Barometer-Executive-Summary.pdf

[6]https://www.slideshare.net/EdelmanInsights/2010-goodpurpose-global-findings-12654442

consumers believe that business should place at least equal weight on society's interests as it does on businesses' interests. More recently, in their 2017 Meaningful Brands study, Havas Media Group indicated that 75 percent of global respondents think that brands should make more of a contribution to our well-being and quality of life. Yet, Americans remain skeptical and continue to raise the bar in terms of expecting businesses and brands to become a part of the solution. For U.S. businesses, improving the world around them, in small or large ways, is no longer an option but increasingly mandatory and embedded in all these businesses do and how they do it.

Each year, multiple studies are published that tout the economic benefits of purpose-driven companies. In their book *People and Profits?* authors Joshua Margolis and Jim Walsh researched over 40 different studies indicating that when treated as an independent variable, corporate social responsibility (CSR) is found to have a positive relationship to financial performance. Of course, there may be companies and brands that purport to be socially conscious yet are only motived by profit; however, here we consider those purpose-based brands that are motivated beyond profit and seek to deliver functionally relevant and emotionally resonant brand experiences. From enterprise-wide CSR efforts all the way down to simply selling a product that makes people a little more confident and even crafting communications that leave people feeling inspired, purpose-driven branding and marketing has been shown to make a difference in both company and employee morale as well as company value and growth. In 2012, research by former Proctor & Gamble marketing chief Jim Stengel, in partnership with global market research firm Millward Brown,[7] revealed that those companies that have committed to and communicated brand ideals such as *brand purpose* grew 3 to 10 times faster than the competition in terms of tangible and intangible value (Figure 4.5). Their research uncovered that the highest-performing companies over a 10-year period—including the height of the recession and known as the *Stengel 50*—all activated their brand purpose in one of five ways:

---

[7] http://www.jimstengel.com/grow/research-validation/

Eliciting Joy: activating experiences of happiness, wonder, and limit-less possibility. Coca-Cola, for example, has made it its mission to "inspire moments of optimism and happiness."

Enabling Connection: enhancing the ability of people to connect with each other and the world in meaningful ways. Facebook's mission statement is to "give people the power to build community and bring the world closer together."

Inspiring Exploration: helping people explore new horizons and new experiences. In their recent campaign, travel booking service Expedia promised to help people find themselves through travel with company tagline, "Find Yours."

Evoking Pride: giving people increased confidence, strength, security, and vitality. Nike's mission statement is "to bring inspiration and innovation to every athlete."

Impacting Society: affecting society broadly, from challenging the status quo to redefining categories. When Method Soap launched chemical-free cleaning products in the United States, they did so by creating a movement called "The People Against Dirty."

In May 2010, business and leadership consultant and author Simon Sinek delivered what is currently the third most viewed TED talk of all

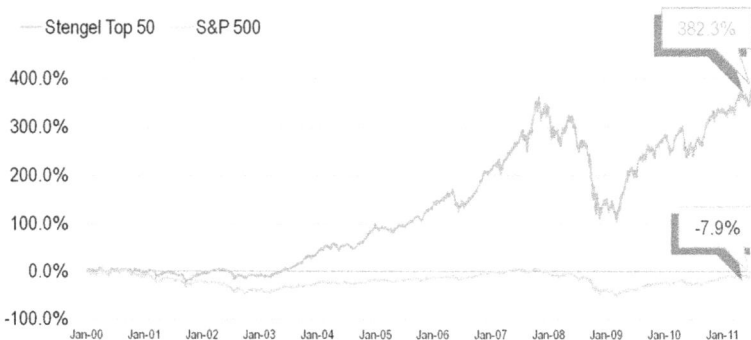

The Stengel 50 vs. S&P 500

Source: Millward Brown Optimor
The 42 publicly traded brands within the top 50 were included in the comparison

Figure 4.5 The Stengel 50, GROW, Jim Stengel, 2011

time entitled, "How great leaders inspire action." Over the course of 18 minutes, Sinek methodically builds the case for why purpose is such an effective motivator when it comes to driving individuals' behavior (a cornerstone of marketing). His approach centers on what he calls the *Golden Circle*, consisting of the following three elements (Figure 4.6):

The What: the products and services a business offers
The How: what makes a business offering (product, service, delivery) special and sets it apart from the competition
The Why: the business purpose, cause, or belief—the reason the organization exists

Sinek points out that most marketers communicate the exact wrong way—from the outside in—with an ineffective focus on functional benefits, features, stats, and facts. For example, an expected message from an uninspired company selling computers would say, "We make great computers; they have enormous memory capacity and the fastest and most powerful processors on the market." Compare this to Apple, whose core promise starts with the why and radiates outward. For example, in his TED talk Sinek states that Apple's "why" would be "because we believe in challenging the status quo and doing things differently is why we make our products beautifully designed and simple to use, we just happen to make great computers." In the end, Sinek offers two salient pieces of advice important for any marketer to consider: (1) The goal is not to do business with everybody who needs what you have. The goal is to do business with people who believe what you believe, and (2) people don't buy *what* you do, they buy *why* you do it.

It's important to note that all brands, both foreign and domestic, need not set out to change the world, although some do. It will suffice if your aim is simply to make the lives of consumers a little bit better

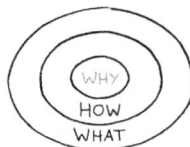

Figure 4.6 Illustration of Simon Sinek Golden Circle

as a result of consuming and interacting with your product and brand. Global advertising agency network Leo Burnett introduced what they refer to as their *HumanKind* philosophy and scale. On their website, they state,

> Creativity has the power to transform human behavior. This is the core belief of what we call HumanKind. It's not about advertising or brand propositions or marketing. It's about people and purpose. It's an approach to marketing that serves true human needs, not the other way around. That's why everything we do for brands is designed with a human purpose in mind. A brand without purpose is one that will never be understood or embraced by people. A brand with purpose can be a true agent of change and transform the way people think, feel or act. A brand with a true Humankind purpose can change the world. Our dream is to be the best creator of those ideas that truly move people—bar none.

The HumanKind 10-point scale seeks to measure the potential impact that a brand's product and messages can have on their business, consumer, communities, and the world. The first four (1 to 4) are deemed to be destructive to the brand and/or a waste of time and effort. The next three (5 to 7) are considered a success by modern marketing standards. The last three (8 to 10) are considered stretch goals, and the truth is that most companies and their agencies will probably never achieve these standards. However, it's certainly worth trying!

1. Destructive
2. No idea
3. Invisible
4. I don't know what the brand stands for
5. I understand the brand's purpose
6. An intelligent idea
7. An inspiring idea, beautifully crafted
8. Changes the way people think and feel
9. Changes the way people live
10. Changes the world

So now what? If yours is a company and brand with a strong sense of mission, vision, and values, you are off to a good start, especially for those brands that are oriented more toward people than profits. Critics of this approach and mind-set might challenge this by stating (using the argument of eminent free-market economists such as Milton Friedman) that ultimately a for-profit company's first and foremost responsibility is to generate profits for its shareholders and stakeholders. Yes, companies must become and remain profitable to keep the lights on and stay in business. Yet, as we've discussed in this chapter, having an orientation to serving people and, with respect to CSR, the greater good has been shown to positively influence profits. Adding to the research examining the benefits of CSR on profitability, the Havas Media Group also looked at more than 1,500 brands in 15 industries and 33 countries and found that *Meaningful Brands*—those identified as having an impact on personal and collective well-being—outperformed the stock market by 206 percent between 2006 and 2016.[8] A helpful starting place for businesses, both large and small, foreign and domestic, is to identify what you believe in and why you exist.

Following are a few examples of brands that have managed to transcend their categories by developing a purpose-based orientation:

Hallmark Greeting Cards
We believe in creating a more emotionally connected world.
We exist to strengthen the health of people's relationships.

Devry University (a for-profit vocational school)
We believe in the value of practical education, not an ornamental one.
We exist to turn thoughts into action, theory into practice and talent into work.

Allstate Insurance
We believe that everyone deserves to live without fear.
We exist to actively protect people every day, not just someday.

---

[8]http://www.meaningful-brands.com/en

With all of the evidence in support of companies with a purpose beyond profit and that are based on brand experiences that stir emotion, this then begs the question, "What is the role of functional benefits in marketing?" After all, in his Golden Circle concept, Simon Sinek made the point that most marketers are focusing on the wrong thing. American author Robert Heinlein nailed it when he wrote, "Man is not a rational animal; he is a rationalizing animal." As it turns out, human decision making tends to be highly irrational and largely unconscious; however, when asked why people make certain decisions, they tend to post-rationalize their decisions using available information to focus on functional benefits. Harvard Business School professor Gerald Zaltman contends that as much as 95 percent of our cognition occurs in the subconscious mind.[9] Linking the power of purpose and emotion in driving decision making with the necessity to provide rational evidence to help consumers support those decisions, consider the following framework that matches what people buy into (the *why*) and the *what* and *how* of the purchase (the product/service itself). It's this powerful combination that helps differentiate your brand:

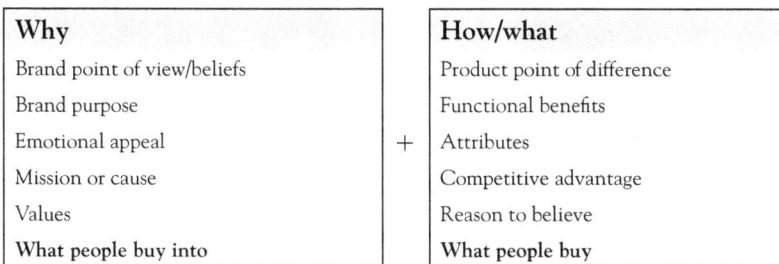

Why		How/what
Brand point of view/beliefs		Product point of difference
Brand purpose		Functional benefits
Emotional appeal	+	Attributes
Mission or cause		Competitive advantage
Values		Reason to believe
What people buy into		**What people buy**

The skillful balance of brand purpose and rational evidence is a hallmark of many of the Unites States' most successful American brands. Following are four examples of this impactful combination of purpose and function and how it informs their overall brand idea as seen in their tagline.

With so much evidence supporting meaningful, purpose-based, and emotionally driven brands, why is it that so many companies remain uninspired and devoid of meaning, purpose, and emotion? Great brands

---

[9]https://hbswk.hbs.edu/item/the-subconscious-mind-of-the-consumer-and-how-to-reach-it

Example	Why		How/what		Brand idea tagline
Coca-Cola	To inspire moments of optimism and happiness		To refresh the world		Open Happiness
Apple	To challenge the status quo and help people create	+	Beautifully designed and simple to use	=	Think Different
Dove	Believes that beauty is more than skin deep, helps give women self-esteem		¼ moisturizing cream, #1 Dermatologist Recommended brand		Real Beauty
Snickers	Prevents you from being "hangry" (hungry and angry)		Packed with peanuts, Snickers satisfies your hunger		You're not you when you're hungry. Snickers satisfies

not only stand for something, but they also stand against things that do not match up with their mission and vision. These are the brands that are on a continual mission to make life better for their customers as well as society. Building a purpose-based brand requires commitment. Crafting an inspired brand that will stand out in the competitive U.S. marketplace is no easy task—it requires research, insight, courage, commitment, and enthusiasm. As something of a litmus test, you can be sure that you are on to a powerful idea if you can answer "yes" to the following four questions:

1. Is it true? Can you actually deliver on what you promise to deliver in your brand and product experience?
2. Is it relevant? Does your brand and product fill an actual need? This can be emotional (in the case of a luxury item like a unique designer handbag) or functional (in the case of a tool such as a new type of screwdriver or superglue).
3. Is it resonant? Is your brand experience emotionally evocative and/ or meaningful to people?

4. Is it different? Is your brand experience unlike anything out there? This can be achieved through purpose, promise, personality, and more.

The lesson here, though, is that to differentiate your product or service in the hypercompetitive U.S. market, it helps to consider the three steps outlined in Figure 4.1: identifying a narrow target audience that you need to attract in order to be successful; making sure your product or service offering aligns with the target in function, design, or messaging; and positioning your offering effectively and strategically versus your competition's.

In the end, people buy brands that they like, that they can wear as a badge, that are aspirational or reflective of their own personal values, and that ultimately make them feel something. Marketers have the opportunity to build brands that mean something, and following Simon Sinek's advice, no longer have to fight for everyone who needs what they have, but rather seek those consumers who believe in what the brand itself believes. More so today than ever, by using modern media channels and tools, marketers can find these people, and one by one, build an army of believers and evangelists.

Questions to Consider

- What are some existing category and competitive conventions that you could potentially disrupt?
- What is your overall positioning? What single-minded idea do you stand for?
- Try writing a few positioning statements. Are they sufficiently focused to help you carve out a distinct territory when considering your competitors?
- As an organization, what are your core values and beliefs? How can these inform your company purpose, beyond profit?
- Which of Stengel's five brand ideals might you be most able to activate? How does this compare with that of your competitors?
- What is your *why*, your *how*, and your *what*? Is there cohesion between what your customers buy versus what they buy into?
- Thinking about the Leo Burnett *HumanKind* scale, how far up the scale would you like to achieve? What actions must be taken in order to accomplish that?

From Planning to Execution: Developing the Marketing Mix

Marketing is a race without a finishing line.
—Philip Kotler (1931–present), author and professor, Kellogg
School of Management

As part of their brand strategy, marketers have long organized their efforts into what's called the *marketing mix*, also known as the 4Ps framework: product (the product or service you're selling, including packaging and design), promotion (your advertising message and other ways to communicate and promote what you're selling, such as discounts, deals, and other promotional offers and events), place (your distribution and retail strategy, where your products are sold and how they reach your customers), and price (your pricing strategy throughout the distribution chain, including retail and wholesale pricing, revenues, costs, and profit margins). The function of marketing is to identify market gaps and develop new products or services accordingly, and your marketing mix enables you to enter new markets through the development or revision of your product, promotion, place, and pricing strategy. Simply put, the components of the marketing mix represent the building blocks of your brand and are designed to deliver value to your customers.

Assuming that you already have some, if not all, of these elements within your domestic market marketing mix, the challenge becomes to determine what elements remain unchanged and which elements must be adapted for entering the U.S. market. One way to approach adapting your marketing mix to entering new markets is to imagine each of the 4Ps as levers that you can pull to develop a more attractive market offering. Moreover, these four levers are dependent on each other, so the change you effect with one lever will most likely influence the other three.

The first step in planning the marketing mix is to begin with your target customer and the compelling reasons why he or she will consider adopting your product (or service) amongst the alternatives in the competitive U.S. market. Nielson Research[10] reports that even given the

---

[10]http://www.nielsen.com/us/en/insights/news/2011/countdown-to-product-launch-12-key-steps.html

millions of dollars companies invest toward developing thousands of new products each year, only 10 percent of these products will end up surviving in the long run. As part of its consumer adoption study, Nielsen tracked hundreds of new product launches. From this study, Nielsen came up with a 12-step process based on the 4Ps outlining key considerations for increasing retail success:

12 Steps to Consumer Adoption

1. Create a unique and distinct product and value proposition to your target audience.
2. Generate attention and interest for the new product.
3. Design the labeling and packaging to communicate shelf appeal to highlight your distinct product and value proposition.
4. Ensure that this message is clearly and concisely communicated at retail.
5. Create a product that serves a definite consumer need.
6. Clearly communicate why your product is different from competing choices.
7. Establish trust and credibility with your brand and product.
8. Know your product limitations and be prepared to address them.
9. Ensure that consumers can find your product (at which retailers and at the store level on the shelves).
10. Establish value related to pricing your product.
11. Ensure that your product delivers the value you promise it will in your advertising and promotions.
12. Build loyal customers to encourage repeat purchases and customer word of mouth.

Product Strategy

Successful products provide attributes and deliver benefits that align with consumer wants and needs. However, when entering a new market such as the United States, brands should view their *product* as more than just the product itself (e.g., how it functions). For instance, product attributes and benefits can be perceived differently depending on consumers' culture, traditions, language, and social factors. The following market entry example illustrates our broadened view of product and is adopted from a recent Harvard Business School case study examining the expansion of a Japanese snack food into the U.S. market.[11]

In 2008, the Kameda Seika (Kameda) brand first launched its #1 selling product, Kakinotane Rice Crackers, in the United States. In market

---

[11]https://hbr.org/product/kameda-seika-cracking-the-us-market/517095-PDF-ENG

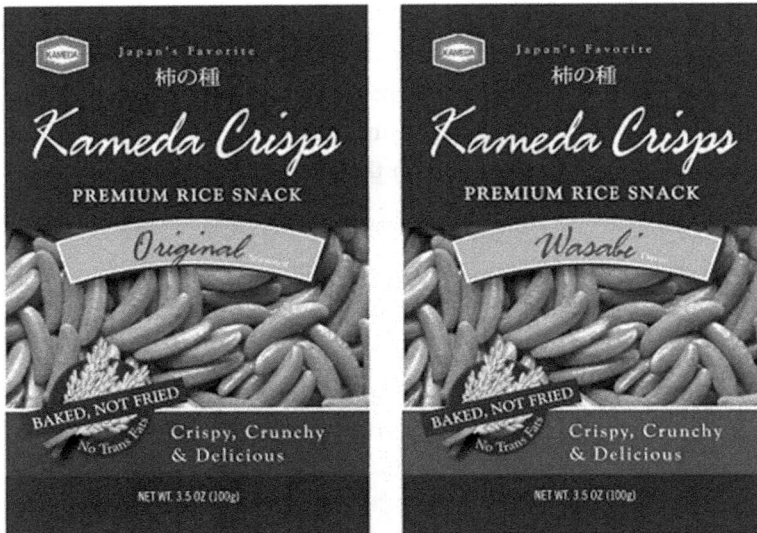

Figure 4.7 Product packaging early in U.S. launch

tests, the brand discovered that the name "Kakinotane" was confusing to American consumers and difficult to pronounce. The product name was subsequently changed to "Kameda Crisps" to better communicate the texture of the chips. To establish a presence in the U.S. grocery market among major chains such as Safeway and Kroger, Kameda first tried promoting its snack crackers with free samples and investing in retail shelf placement (called slotting fees). However, demand for the new crackers was initially disappointing, and Kameda decided to shift its distribution to higher-end retailers such as Gelson's and Whole Foods in the Western United States—a region with a significant Asian American population. Finally, as part of its long-term market entry strategy, Kameda redesigned its product packaging (Figures 4.7 and 4.8), shifting the focus away from prominently promoting the brand name and instead highlighting the cracker's unique flavors and crunchy experience. Because of the successful evolution of its market entry strategy over time, Kamada Crisps are now sold throughout the United States.

The important point with the Kameda Crisp launch is that over time the brand began to widen its view of the product, beyond its functional form, to consider packaging and messaging and how the packaging

Figure 4.8 Product packaging in 2017

communicated the benefits of the crackers in a visual and emotional approach. This ties to what marketing experts refer to as the key elements to differentiating your brand, including package design (color, shape, function, materials); engaging the senses through sight, sound, smell, touch, even taste; and creating a unique shopping or consumption experience.

Depending on product type, another factor to consider when developing product strategy is the product adoption life cycle among your market's consumers (Figure 4.9). Especially for technology-based products such as smartphones and other mobile devices or electronic cars, knowing how to reach and convince those innovators and early adopters that your product is the next best thing can be critical to ultimately reaching and selling to the larger market and late adopters—the early and late majority consumers and laggards.

One example of U.S. market entry and product adoption involves Australian wines and an innovation in the wine bottling process. Ever since the 18th century, wine bottles have been sealed by a cork. Throughout the years, it has become a tradition to open a fine wine with a corkscrew, particularly in more expensive restaurants as the sommelier uncorks the

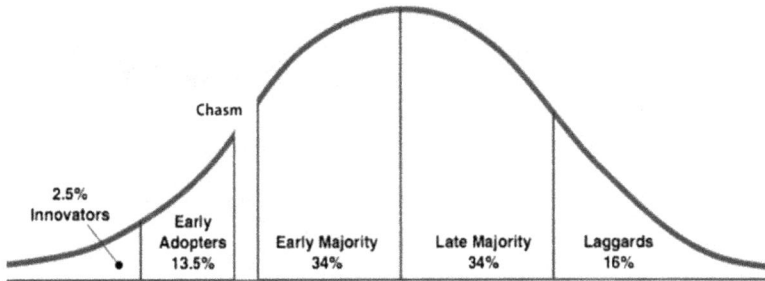

Figure 4.9 Product life cycle

bottle of Merlot at the table with a flourish. However, today in Australia, 99 out of every 100 bottles of wine produced are sealed not with a cork but with a screw top, or screwcap.[12] Australian winemakers, researchers, and scientists had recently discovered that innovating with a screwcap led to less batches of wine spoiled through cork rot and taint, resulting in greater consistency of wines bottled and sold. Despite its success in Australia, this innovation in wine bottling has not yet taken hold within markets such as the United States, where wine drinkers still hold on to traditions such as the ritual opening of the wine bottle with a corkscrew and where these wine drinkers also hold attitudes and beliefs that corked wines are superior. In the face of, or ignorant of, evidence that screwcaps make for a better (and easier) wine drinking experience, innovators and early adopters such as restaurants and retail stores have resisted this innovation, characteristic of the laggard segment of the product life cycle, and this resistance has diminished the spread of screwcap wines to the larger U.S. market.

Finally, another consideration when developing a market entry strategy around a product or service is to what degree does the entrant standardize its product offerings or adapt and change its offerings to meet the needs, attitudes, culture, and behaviors of the new market. For example, McDonald's operates over 33,000 restaurants in almost 120 countries. For McDonald's to totally customize its menu and food items to each market or country would not only be financially and operationally

---

[12]http://www.smh.com.au/business/australias-wine-screwcap-revolution-20170628-gx0e3l.html

impossible, but would also risk McDonald's losing central elements of its marketing mix and appeal in some markets, including its iconic Big Mac and Golden Arches. However, because food is so closely tied to local culture, McDonald's operates a hybrid standardized/customized product strategy that retains iconic menu items around the world yet also develops new items, such as the McSpicy Paneer in India, and distribution methods like scooter delivery in Korea. Because there is no one-size-fits-all model for determining the degree of standardization or customization for market entry, the objective of SMEs when entering a large market such as the United States should be to retain what is essential to the brand while at the same time developing new products to appeal to local or regional tastes.

In the next section, we discuss the second P, promotion, and ways that companies and brands can most effectively and efficiently communicate product and service features, benefits, and innovations (such as innovations in wine bottling with screwcaps) to consumers.

Promotion and Communication

The second P in the marketing mix, promotion, involves strategically communicating with your consumer with the right message, to the right person, at the right place, at the right time. Marketing professor Jef Richards argued, "Creative without strategy is called 'art.' Creative with strategy is called 'advertising.'" Beautiful and cinematic advertising creative work may win you awards; it may not, however, help you win the hearts and minds (and wallets) of your target consumer. How and where you communicate with your consumer, with your overall market entry strategy in mind, is the focus of this section.

Broadly speaking, communication strategies available to SMEs entering the U.S. market involve traditional and digital advertising, sales promotion (e.g., incentives, coupons), and direct selling and marketing. Communicating with the right message means being sensitive to the cultural factors that can act as barriers to making sure your message is understood by consumers in a new market. Being in the right place at the right time involves understanding what we call the *customer journey*. It begins with establishing an awareness among your target audience that your brand

and product simply exist. Once you establish awareness and enter your customer's consideration set (the set of products or brands that he or she might consider purchasing), the customer journey evolves to one of information gathering and evaluation of a smaller set of alternatives, sometimes called the *evoked set,* and where consumers develop an interest in what you have to offer. Unlike the traditional marketing funnel, the consumer decision journey (Figure 4.10) is a loop, ideally resulting in repeat purchase. Smart marketers pursue target-specific media touchpoints and relevant messaging specifically tailored for each stage of the journey.

Promotions and advertising strategies can be characterized by two different approaches to communicating your message: (1) a push strategy and (2) a pull strategy. A push strategy emphasizes personal selling and direct company–consumer interactions. A pull strategy emphasizes traditional as well as digital and social media advertising. Ultimately, whether through push or pull communications, consumers move from this interest stage to desire and conviction that your product is the right one for them, whether it's a candy bar or a car, although these two product categories involve a significantly different amount of cognitive effort and depth of information gathering and processing leading to purchase. On the one hand, a candy bar purchase most likely takes place with minimal cognitive effort and involvement and may indeed represent a mindless, impulsive purchase in the store check-out aisle. On the other hand, a

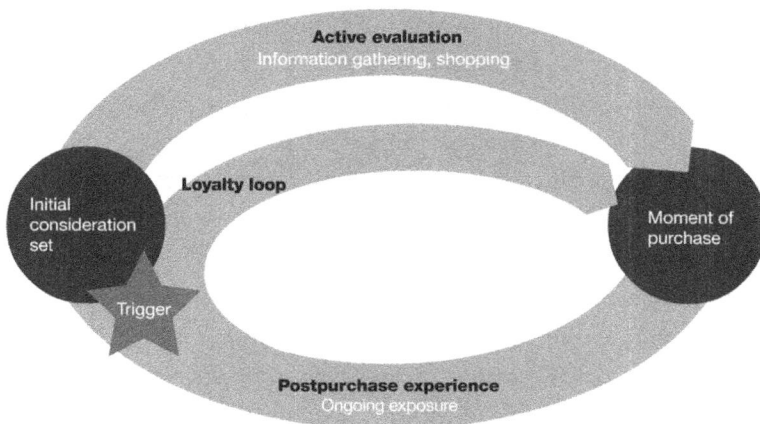

Figure 4.10 McKinsey consumer decision journey

car purchase most likely involves weeks if not months of online research across multiple information sources (car brand websites, magazines such as *Car and Driver*, as well as other commercial platforms such as Kelley Blue Book, Autotrader, and Cars.com) and visits to local car dealers.

Looking back to the 1960s and 70s, brand and product advertising throughout the customer journey involved a relatively limited selection of media: television, magazines, radio, newspapers, and out-of-home (e.g., billboards, street kiosks). Today, the media landscape is more complex and is populated with traditional media (including television) as well as an enormous variety of digital and online media. Websites, social media (including Facebook, Instagram, Snapchat, and Twitter), online content providers (e.g., YouTube), search advertising (primarily through Google Adwords), and even mobile video games are just some of the media alternatives that make up the online advertising landscape.

In fact, research suggests that almost 7 in 10 actions within the customer journey include accessing online reviews and word-of-mouth recommendations from others. These reviews and customer-to-customer interactions primarily take place on social media, especially among younger consumers. Additionally, recent studies have shown that Gen Z and Millennials are influenced to a far greater extent by social media such as Facebook and Snapchat when making purchase decisions than are older consumer segments such as Baby Boomers.[13] It's notable that just two digital advertising platforms—Google and Facebook—represent 50 percent of the world's digital advertising. It makes sense that brands should align their advertising and media spending where consumers access information, and therefore these two platforms are a good place to start if you are a foreign SME seeking to build awareness in the U.S. market.

In terms of online advertising content, one notable trend is toward the growth of video advertising on social media such as Facebook and Snapchat.[14] Spending on digital and mobile video increased 67 percent from 2015 through 2017 as more and more brands tap into online video-based

---

[13]D. Daye. "Ways to Differentiate Your Brand," https://www.brandingstrategyinsider .com/2013/12/50-ways-to-differentiate-your-brand.html

[14]https://www.emarketer.com/Article/How-Social-Platforms-Using-Video-Capture-Audience-Attention/1016362?ecid=NL1009

advertising options from platforms such as Facebook, Instagram, Snapchat, and YouTube.[15] Remembering the adage of being in the right place at the right time with the right message and content, it's important to recognize that young consumers are spending more and more time on their smartphones viewing video content, and that's why brands are investing more in the mobile space. Moreover, as we discussed earlier, research also indicates that younger consumers' attention spans have today fallen to less than five seconds, shorter than that of the average goldfish.[16]

One important trend influencing how brands advertise and promote in the United States is the growth in the use of mobile devices such as smartphones and the extent that these devices are used for access to content and social media. (The *Economist* recently reported that Americans physically tap or swipe their phones on the average of 2,600 times per day.) One of the authors of this book referred to the mobile marketing phenomenon as *brand in the hand* in portraying the opportunities mobile devices bring to companies seeking to reach consumers in the context of their daily lives and routines. In order to leverage the power of mobile marketing, brands today must have, at the very least, mobile compatible websites with the addition of mobile apps that add value by enabling mobile shopping and payments, promoting loyalty programs, tracking deliveries, and offering location-based promotions, coupons, and incentives. With over 70 percent of the U.S. population owning and using a smartphone from morning to night, and even sleeping with their phones, brands seeking to enter the U.S. market must build and maintain a mobile presence.

The POEM Framework. An important dimension of any advertising and promotion strategy involves media choice and spending. Because the universe of media alternatives has exploded in recent years with online and social media sources, one helpful model in planning your media is called the POEM framework, with the P standing for paid media, the O standing for owned media, and the E standing for earned media.

---

[15]https://www.iab.com/wp-content/uploads/2017/05/2017-IAB-NewFronts-Video-Ad-Spend-Report.pdf

[16]https://www.mediapost.com/publications/article/306007/pay-attention-quickly.html

Paid media is just that—traditional media such as television, print, as well as online and social media that you pay for. In many ways and for many reasons, paid online and social media is the first type of media that SMEs should consider when launching an advertising program or campaign. First, social media such as Facebook enables robust audience targeting. Leveraging Facebook tools such as Facebook Pages (over 70 million businesses now operate these branded Facebook profiles) and paid advertising through boosted posts that target custom audiences, marketers can more efficiently and effectively reach specific customer segments than possible with traditional media. Along with the rapid growth of businesses advertising on the Facebook platform, advertising rates (as measured by CPM or the cost to reach one thousand individuals) have almost tripled since 2016. Still, in terms of media spending efficiency, Facebook's current CPM rates (around $11 to $12) are still attractive compared with traditional media, and its targeting capabilities make it effective for reaching specific audience types.

Facebook also conducts what it calls Facebook Blueprint, an online learning platform where individuals can take courses in areas such as campaign development and building reach and awareness. Within the customer journey, Facebook advertising is particularly beneficial for the interest and affinity building stages.

Snapchat (Snap Inc.) is an upstart social media platform and is the most widely used social media among teens in the United States. With its tool called Ad Manager for SMEs, advertisers can buy ads on Snap with credit cards in an auction-based bidding system, similar to Google's paid search platform called AdWords. For awareness building, Google's AdWords platform (a paid search tool) is the dominant tool in the United States for SMEs seeking to appear prominently on search results. The AdWords platform enables businesses to bid on certain keywords and phrases in order to appear on Google search results pages. Paid search is also an important form of advertising since mobile search is now the fastest growing area in terms of search behavior. Factors influencing search results placement include keyword bids, the relevance of the keywords to the business and its website, and other factors included in a sophisticated algorithm developed by Google to insure that the most relevant search results will appear given a respective search term.

Another benefit of paid online media is how online media enables businesses to behaviorally *retarget* customers who have previously searched for or visited a company's website with online ads (banners, videos) when they visit other websites. For instance, if someone searched for the "new Lebron James Nike shoe" on Google, he might also begin to see Nike ads appearing on other websites he visits. Retargeting is an effective and efficient form of paid online advertising because it helps businesses reach out to people who they can assume are interested in specific products based on their recent online behaviors and actions.

Owned media includes company mobile apps and website; content that is produced and distributed by the brand on channels like YouTube (sometimes called *branded content*); the company's social presence on Facebook, Twitter, Instagram; and other online content such as blogs. Owned media and paid media work hand in hand to connect consumers to company-owned and -managed assets, such as in the case where paid search and social media advertising drives traffic to the company's website or mobile presence.

Earned media occurs when individuals and customers share, post, forward, and retweet social media content or post reviews related to your company, brand, or product. It can also include press articles generated through public relations efforts. Remembering that we discussed how younger consumers (Millennials and Gen Z) are skeptical toward advertising in general, earned media can be an effective form of promotion because individuals are more likely to believe what others outside of your company say about your product than what you say. For good reason, some call earned media the *holy grail* of advertising and promotion.

Influencer marketing is also a form of earned media. Although you may develop satisfied and delighted customers who serve as brand ambassadors—willingly recommending your products to others at no cost to you—influencer marketing is increasingly a popular form of paid and earned media. For instance, the professional football player Cristiano Ronaldo, because of his social media following and appeal built with millions of fans worldwide, can be paid millions of dollars per Instagram post for brands in product categories such as shoes and watches, and other celebrities such as Kim Kardashian get paid substantial amounts for social media posts glowing about the latest face cream. The research firm Keller Fay defines an influencer as a person who has greater-than-average reach or impact through word of mouth in a relevant market-place. Influencer marketing can include promoting products or services to influencers to increase brand awareness or promoting the same products or services through influencers (such as the case with athletes such as Ronaldo or celebrities such as one of the Kardashians). A-list celebrities are not the only option either; more and more marketers are looking to what they call *micro-influencers,* those who share knowledge and opinion on a smaller scale. Another reason why influencers are a growing form of brand advertising and promotion relates back to the product life cycle discussed earlier in this chapter. Author Geoffrey Moore, in his book *Crossing the Chasm*, suggests that to reach mass market adoption, marketers should first focus on those innovators and early adopters. In turn, these early adopters and innovators will influence the early and late majority consumers and even the laggards.

Beyond paid influencers, another common approach employed by savvy marketers is to activate earned media by leveraging the news media through PR efforts. For example, in November 2017, e-commerce floral delivery service Teleflora installed a physical wall of flowers called the *Wall of Love* in front of the U.S. government Capitol building in Washington D.C. The 50-foot wide and 8-foot high barrier contained 1,300 handmade floral bouquets, each with Teleflora branding on the holder. The flowers were meant to be taken by passersby and once all removed, the wall revealed the message, "Love Out Loud." The provocative activation was not only on-brand for Teleflora, but was also picked up by a multitude of news sources and bloggers due to the relevance of its message during a time of deep political unrest in the United States. This coverage by the press extended Teleflora's brand message much further than an equivalent traditional advertising investment would have afforded the brand.

Place and Distribution

When discussing the third P, place, the first company that often comes up in conversation is Amazon. The U.S. retail market is heavily concentrated among a few large retailers, one of which is Amazon. More than any other company (at least in the United States), Amazon has revolutionized the way products are moved through the distribution system to reach its customers. The point of this section, though, is not to cover Amazon's sophisticated network of warehouses and distribution centers and delivery platforms, but to emphasize the growth and importance of e-commerce and online retail in the U.S. market where customers have grown accustomed to one-click ordering and rapid, almost instantaneous, delivery. We also need to emphasize the role of physical retail within American culture—the death of the shopping mall but the resurgence of the physical retail experience in other retail outlets. For example, Amazon recently purchased the national grocery chain Whole Foods and its 400 or so stores throughout the United States for almost $14 billion. For Amazon, the acquisition of Whole Foods serves two purposes: First, it helps fulfill Amazon's Prime Now promise of same-day delivery for items such as groceries, and second, it helps to solidify Amazon's presence as the retailer of, well, everything.

So, to succeed within the U.S. retail market, one has to consider Amazon's footprint and be prepared to be better, faster, or different (because to be cheaper may not be a sustainable proposition). This was the case, before Amazon's recent developments and acquisitions, with a Brazilian eyewear and accessory brand, Chilli Beans.[17] Chilli Beans had grown to be a successful brand in Latin America since the mid-1990s through its franchise retail stores and kiosks that emphasized self-service and encouraged customers to try on its sunglasses without having to find a retail associate to open a locked case in a traditional store. However, when it entered the U.S. market, Chilli Beans discovered that American consumers perceived products sold through free-standing kiosks, a primary mode of distribution for the company in other countries, as lower quality. American consumers also had become conditioned to the convenience of shopping online and to shop for discounts. To enter the U.S. market with physical retail stores was going to be too costly for Chilli Beans—where each kiosk might cost $20,000 to open and where retail stores could cost $1.5 million each. In response to the countervailing trends of prohibitive retail investment and the propensity for American consumers to shop

---

[17]Chilli Beans HBS Case: http://www.hbs.edu/faculty/Pages/item.aspx?num=50333

online, Chilli Beans moved aggressively into e-commerce, with its CEO remarking that "it's impossible not to have an online store now." Chilli Beans in the United States has since evolved to an omnichannel retail strategy, opening physical flagship stores in key markets such as Southern California while at the same time growing its e-commerce business.

For many brands and retailers competing in the U.S. market, and to meet the demands for low prices, convenient shopping, and breadth of product selection, it is indeed impossible today not to have an online presence. For many well-established retailers in the United States, their shift to e-commerce came either too late or has been overshadowed by losses in the physical retail space. In 2017 alone, nine major U.S. retailers have gone bankrupt; iconic brands such as: J.C. Penney, Macy's, Radio Shack, and Sears have closed hundreds of stores; and The Sports Authority, one of the first major sporting goods chains in the United States, closed its doors for good. Although overall retail sales in the United States continue to grow, consumers are buying more online and the physical retail landscape is cluttered with an overabundance of shopping malls. Further, consumer spending is shifting from a purely transactional, product-based mind-set to one of experiences through restaurants, bars, and travel.

Given the shifting retail landscape in the United States, there are numerous retail strategies available for brands entering the U.S. market, depending on the product or service. Whereas e-commerce is a must, market entrants involved in retail should also look for critical markets in which to open some type of retail presence, even though the development of *pop-up* stores, a retail strategy that leverages unused or vacant retail space to establish a temporary presence in a specific market.

Pricing Strategy

Pricing, the fourth and final P, is the one element of your marketing mix that directly influences demand and profitability. Depending on the market and the product offering, your pricing strategy may be affected by what we call *price elasticity of demand*. For example, demand for your products is elastic when a small change in price results in a large change in demand. Conversely, demand is inelastic when a large change in price results in only a small shift in demand. As such, it is important to develop pricing strategy according to your desired market positioning and product offering, your competition, and your target audience's perception of value. One company that mastered this approach is Deutsch Family Wine and Spirits as it entered the complex and fickle U.S. market with its Yellow Tail brand of wine. When Yellow Tail was introduced in the U.S. market, Australian wines accounted for less than 5 percent of all U.S. wine imports. Yet within 10 years after its launch, Yellow Tail had achieved mass distribution in the United States and had become one of the most popular wines among casual wine drinkers by following a value-based pricing strategy. Besides Yellow Tail's specially engineered wine formulation that appealed to a wide swath of U.S. wine drinkers (not too sophisticated, yet simple and soft to the taste), its unique labeling featured a colorful wallaby and its pricing was affordable to the masses at less than $10 a bottle.

Ultimately, your pricing strategy will be about delivering value to your customers, where value is the difference between the extent to which your product benefits your end user and how much it cost him or her to buy it. And in some cases, as with the Yellow Tail launch, there are numerous pricing strategies, and all are dependent on your market, your brand and product offering, and your consumer's willingness to pay. Yellow Tail followed an *economy pricing* strategy, delivering value (a good tasting wine) at a price lower than competing wine labels. Similar to an economy pricing strategy is a *market penetration pricing* strategy, where the company introduces a product or service with pricing below market in order to generate sales and penetrate the market. A *premium pricing* strategy is one that positions your product as relatively higher priced yet also offering relatively greater value (in terms of quality, prestige, and status). Some refer to this as *pricing with pride*, and it is central to how venerable brands such as Starbucks or Cathay Pacific develop their pricing strategies. Following a *parity pricing* strategy, your product would be priced at parity with your competition in the hopes that some supplemental element of your business (for instance, customer service and support) will help differentiate your offerings. A *price skimming* strategy is one where initially your product is priced at a premium level (at or above your competition) to attract those customers who want to be the first among their peers or in their network to own it (e.g., innovators or early adopters), in effect building profit margins, and then over time the price is reduced to penetrate a greater portion of your market. Finally, *price bundling* is a strategy where two compatible or complimentary products are sold together with a bundled price for the two. Oftentimes, this occurs with items such as shampoo and conditioner or with cable television, Internet, and phone service packages, where the individual products can be used together. Bundled pricing approaches are also useful when they convey the perception of value or when they help sell excess inventory.

It is important to note that each of these pricing strategies involves trade-offs. Premium pricing can maximize profits yet reduce sales volume. Economy or market penetration pricing can boost sales yet cut into profits. Again, when determining the best pricing strategy for market entry, it's important to consider how you want to be positioned in the market, how it relates to your product or service offering, how your pricing compares with your competition's, how it effects your sales volume and forecasts as well as profit margins, and how it coincides with your target audience's perception of value.

Questions to Consider

- What are the key elements from your brand that you must retain in order to build global recognition?
- How, if at all, might you adapt your product to better suit the marketplace wants and needs?
- In thinking about your customer's decision journey, what are the most relevant media touchpoints and messages for each stage (trigger, consideration, information gathering/shopping, purchase, postpurchase, and loyalty)?
- Considering the prominence of video and influencers (large and small), how might you leverage them to help build awareness in order to cross over into mass market adoption?
- What is your distribution strategy? Is it purely online or a mix of physical and online, and what is your associated pricing strategy? How will you satisfy the increasing demand for a unique brand experience as well as deliver on the high expectations for variety, speed, and customer service?

Marketing Analytics: Measure, Test, Learn, Optimize

I think it's very important to have a feedback loop, where you're constantly thinking about what you've done and how you could be doing it better. I think that's the single best piece of advice: constantly think about how you could be doing things better and questioning yourself.

—Elon Musk (1971–present), South African–born investor, engineer, inventor, and businessman.

In the early 2000s, the German car brand BMW launched a series of short six- to nine-minute films called *BMWFilms*. In the film series, starring well-known actors such as Clive Owen and directed by top-shelf Hollywood talent, BMW sought to promote its 3, 5, and 7 series models to a younger audience of future luxury car buyers. In addition to its unique branded content, one other unique factor of the film series was that the content was distributed exclusively online. This meant that individuals who wished to view the films had to register at bmw.com in order to download the films (remember, the campaign was released prior to YouTube and video streaming technology).

Although it might seem a cumbersome way to get consumers to view content, the fact that the films were released, downloaded, and viewed exclusively online provided BMW North America a treasure chest of data and information about the films' viewership as well as the viewers themselves. BMW was able to track metrics such as the number of individuals registered to view the films, the total number of film views, as well as brand metrics such as BMW purchase intent and brand favorability over time. Because of the online distribution of the films, BMW used the online viewership data to favorably compare media spending on a cost-per-thousand (viewers) basis with more traditional media such as television. The BMWFilms campaign was one of the first marketing campaigns conducted exclusively online—and one of the first marketing examples that highlights the changing nature of how companies and their brands measure advertising effectiveness.

Marketing executives have long struggled with measuring the performance of their marketing activity, particularly before the emergence of online and digital media. The retail executive, John Wanamaker, foreshadowed these challenges back in the 1920s with his appeal for better methods to measure and test the effectiveness of marketing activities such as advertising—where measuring and testing could help managers learn and optimize their marketing investments. Wanamaker famously stated, "Half the money I spend on advertising is wasted; the trouble is I don't know which half." This process of measuring, testing, learning, and optimization shown in Figure 4.11—what we call *marketing analytics*—is as or more important today as it was decades ago before the Internet and when media *dinosaurs* roamed the earth (in the form of magazines, newspapers, radio broadcasts, and even television commercials).

Even as recent as the 1970s, the advertising media landscape in the United States was made up of only three television networks from which advertisers could choose: CBS, NBC, and ABC. A handful of magazines ruled the print media landscape, including *Time, Newsweek, Better Homes and Gardens*, and *Sports Illustrated*. Newspapers, delivered to your door once a day by the neighborhood kid on a bike, were also a prime source of advertising content. Although the number of advertising outlets were relatively sparse compared with today, measuring the effectiveness of these outlets proved elusive because it was difficult if not impossible to track these offline media vehicles' influence on how and where we shopped and what we bought. Now, marketers benefit (as did BMW) from being able to measure consumers' online activity, including access to and consumption of branded content and actual website and e-commerce activity and online sales.

Marketing analytics—the measurement and tracking of key data and metrics (e.g., market size, sales, customer acquisition and retention, website

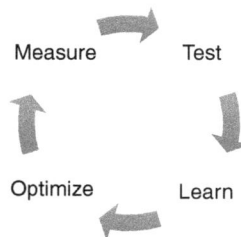

Figure 4.11 Feedforward optimization loop

and social media activity)—helps businesses optimize and maximize their marketing mix strategy and execution. Today, companies and brands focus their analytics efforts on metrics such as customer engagement, a metric that is central to both online and offline marketing strategy. Imagine the number of ways companies engage their customers. For instance, Apple engages its customers with its website, its iTunes store, and its beautifully designed retail stores. Amazon engages its customers with its extensive online product offerings, its Amazon Prime service, and the original entertainment content it produces through its studio division. The point is, your interactions with your current and prospective customers provide a vast amount of data available to measure, test, learn from, and use to optimize your marketing efforts. On the one hand, if alive today an executive like Wanamaker might find comfort in the newfound ability to measure and track his shoppers' activity. At the same time, he might scratch his head in confusion over how to manage and analyze these vast amounts of data.

That is what this chapter is about: to highlight methods and offer guidance on how managers of SMEs can learn to harness and analyze the potentially vast amount of data available to them about their customers and their online and offline behavior. Let's start with the things you should be measuring and how you can measure them. The important first step in developing your analytics plan is to begin to define your key performance indicators, or KPIs. KPIs are important measures because they illustrate the health of your business, such as sales, sales conversions from website visits, market share, loyalty, return on advertising spending, and future purchase intent. Note that this is just a short list of possible KPIs; yours will depend on your unique business and marketing context. An effective and simple approach to identifying KPIs with respect to online data involves categorizing them into three buckets and tracking them over time: (1) reach (the volume of individuals you are reaching with, for instance, your social media presence), (2) engagement (what specific interactions are occurring between you and these individuals online), and (3) your website and social media activity as well as sales volume, market share, and profit margins.

Your KPIs are the higher-level measures that help you measure and track your business and marketing activity and performance. Metrics are those specific measures that are the building blocks of your KPIs. Online metrics can include social media interactions such as Facebook or Instagram shares, likes, posts, and comments; click-through rates (CTRs) driving customers from your social media or search platforms such as Google or Bing to your website; as well as Twitter comments and retweets. Metrics can also include website activity such as page views, time spent on web pages, new visitors, website traffic sources (where your visitors came from), website navigation pathways, conversion rates (e.g., from web page to purchase), and even bounce rate (measured by how much time they spend on your site, or the percentage of visitors that left your site after viewing only one page).

Analytics Platforms

To help with this analysis, there a number of free native analytics platforms, including Facebook Insights, Instagram Analytics, Twitter Analytics, and Google Analytics. Facebook Insights provides a user-friendly dashboard that reports and tracks metrics such as Page Likes, Post Reach, and Engagement activity. Instagram Analytics helps you track your top posts, mentions and followers, audience reach, as well as the extent to which your Instagram audience is engaging with you. Twitter Analytics reports and tracks your tweet activity and followers. Google Analytics helps to bridge your social media presence and activity with your website activity by tracking, among many other metrics, the demographics of your visitors, whether they are new or returning visitors, sources of your website traffic, and the navigation pathways visitors take on your website. Google Analytics also helps you track total website visits over time, number of pages viewed, time spent on each page, and bounce rate. Google has similar native analytics dashboards for YouTube called YouTube Analytics and for Google AdWords called AdWords Analytics.

For instance, if you are developing a paid search campaign using Google AdWords to help consumers who are searching for information on relevant products or services to find you during their online search, AdWords provides a native analytics platform to help you track the effectiveness of your paid search campaign, helping you track impressions, CTRs, and conversions based on specific keywords or groups of keywords.

Imagine that to promote the book that you are reading here on how small and medium size companies can effectively enter foreign markets such as the United States, the authors might develop an AdWords campaign and bid on the keywords *market entry book, foreign SMEs*, and *U.S. market entry* in order to get their book placed high on the Google search results pages related to those search terms. AdWords Analytics would then help them track the effectiveness and costs associated with their paid search campaign. And when you combine Google Analytics with your AdWords account, you can learn even more about your customers' activity on your website after clicking on your paid search ad.

Optimization Techniques

Given the breadth of online data at (literally) your fingertips, analysis of these data can help companies optimize their marketing efforts and spending by testing the effectiveness of paid social (e.g., Facebook advertising) and paid search (e.g., Google AdWords) campaigns. One optimization approach is called A/B testing. Applying A/B testing, a brand can test the relative performance of two different versions of the same entity (e.g., a web page, social media post, mobile app) by varying the content across a control and a variation of the control.

For example, imagine you are a small start-up women's fashion brand entering the U.S. market and you're wondering what type of promotional e-mails you should send out as you build your mailing list. In an A/B test, you would create a control e-mail with a subject line, headline, visual, and copy (we'll call it e-mail A) as well as a variation of that control e-mail, changing one piece of the content, say the visual, in your variation e-mail (we'll call it e-mail B). In your control e-mail, you feature an image of one your dresses on a mannequin and in your variation e-mail you feature the same dress, but worn by a model and not on a mannequin. A/B testing would then allow you to learn from real-time data and feedback by examining metrics such as e-mail open rate and conversions (from e-mail open rates to website visits to website purchases) across your control and variation e-mails. You could then continue testing other pieces of content one at a time (such as descriptive dress copy or headlines) in your subsequent versions of both control and variation e-mails and apply your results to conducting further A/B tests in an iterative approach. In the same way, this same approach could be used to optimize your Facebook posts by varying visuals, headlines, and copy across control and variation social media posts.

A simplified step-by step approach to optimization using A/B testing involves[18] the following:

1. Analyze the data and decide on that specific piece of content or entity you want to improve and optimize. It might be a web page with low-conversion or high-bounce rates or an underperforming Facebook post.
2. Identify your specific objective(s), ranging from increasing CTRs to website visits-to-sales conversions.
3. Create variations in your web page, social media post, or other entity that you are testing.
4. Test, learn, and apply the results in an iterative approach to optimizing your content.

Analytics Scorecards

As we've highlighted thus far in this chapter, marketing analytics involves more than simply collecting and measuring data. It also involves making sense of the data and the metrics that you are measuring by benchmarking and tracking key metrics over time. One approach to measuring your social media or website effectiveness is to develop a custom *scorecard*[19] that captures and tracks key metrics. An example of a brand's social media scorecard, shown in Figure 4.12, highlights how it (1) identifies key metrics to be measured and tracked (such as Facebook likes and Twitter posts), (2) captures the volume of activity for each of these metrics, (3) adds in a multiplier (from 0 to 1) indicating the relative importance or weight of these metrics aligned with your established business objectives, (4) calculates a metric-specific number multiplying the volume of

---

[18]https://www.optimizely.com/optimization-glossary/ab-testing/

[19]A. Rohm, and M. Weiss. 2014. *Herding Cats: A Strategic Approach to Social Media Marketing*. New York, NY: Business Experts Press.

Metrics	# Items	Social media multiplier	Total	Overall total
FB likes	1,000	0.1	100	
FB comments/shares	5,000	0.3	1,500	
Twitter posts	30	0.1	3	
YouTube video views	10	0.4	4	
Blog posts	20	0.4	8	
Website visits over 1:00(minute)	10,000	0.3	3,000	
Pinterest favorites	50	0.5	25	4,640

Figure 4.12 A social media scorecard

activity and the multiplier effect, and (5) reports a (weekly or monthly) overall total scorecard score. In Figure 4.12, the scorecard indicates an overall total of 4,640, which on its own, doesn't tell us much. However, tracking your scorecard scores over time can help you identify the growth or decline of your social media presence, given the metrics and their relative importance that you have identified as critical to your success.

You could also develop a similar scorecard template for tracking your website activity and performance over time by substituting metrics such as website visits, percentage of new visitors, pages viewed, time spent on site, and both conversion and bounce rates for your social media metrics. Doing so, whether for tracking social media or website activity, can help you—in the spirit of analytics—make sense of your data, identify areas of strength and weakness, and optimize!

Online Listening

Depending on the scope of your social media presence and budget, there are some powerful online listening tools available that help companies and brands monitor their social media presence and online activity. For instance, a firm entering the crowded and competitive fast-food space in the United States could use fee- or subscription-based services such as Netbase, Radian6, or Sysomos to monitor social media activity (e.g., posts, comments, shares, mentions, sentiment) across platforms such as Facebook, Instagram, Snapchat, and Twitter related to the brand

and its competitors based on factors such as geography. Innovative brands, large and small, often use tools such as these to study the influence of social media activity on sales.

Whatever your product or service and market entry strategy, it is our hope that applying the concept of analytics to harnessing and making sense of the significant volume of data available (and in many cases easily accessed via native [and free] analytics platforms such as Facebook Insights and Google Analytics) can help you measure and test the effectiveness of your marketing activities and optimize your marketing investments.

Questions to Consider

- In thinking about your marketing objectives and strategies, what are your most important KPIs and associated metrics to help you measure success?
- Similarly, what analytics platforms are most relevant to your overall business objectives and strategies?
- What are some opportunities for you to test, learn, and optimize your marketing efforts with A/B testing?

About the Authors

Anatoly Zhuplev is a professor of international business and entrepreneurship at Loyola Marymount University and former editor-in-chief at the *Journal of East West Business* (2011 to 2013). He taught for 10 years at the Moscow Management Institute and subsequently at the Advanced Training Institute of the State Committee for Printing and Publishing in Moscow; in Bonn, Germany in 1994, 1998, 2009; in Warsaw, Poland (as a Fulbright scholar) in 2005; in Paris, France from 2004to 2007; and at Northeastern University in Boston, Massachusetts from 1989 to 1990. His books, book chapters, and articles on international management, international entrepreneurship, international business, European energy security, and corporate governance (around 100 overall) have been published in the United States, Canada, Western Europe, Russia, and the former USSR. He received his PhD from the Moscow Management Institute, Russia, in 1981, and his BS from the Moscow Engineer-Economics Institute in 1974.

Matthew Stefl joined Loyola Marymount University's College of Business Administration in 2014 as clinical professor and codirector of the M-School program. Matt brings with him over 17 years of advertising industry experience, most recently acting as executive vice president, director of strategic planning at Los Angeles-based Dailey & Associates. Prior to Dailey, he held various roles at agencies like RPA, RAPP, and DDB and has touched nearly every aspect of the business from media planning to copywriting to digital marketing to strategic planning. Matt also draws from a diverse résumé of experience while working with some of the world's biggest companies and brands like Google, Wonderful Company, Honda, Toyota, Turbo Tax, Nestlé, Dole, Bank of America, Wells Fargo, and many more. In addition to teaching, he enjoys a variety of consulting opportunities throughout the year.

Andrew (Andy) Rohm is professor of marketing within the College of Business Administration at Loyola Marymount University (LMU) in Los Angeles, California. Professor Rohm earned his BS in aerospace engineering from the University of Michigan and his PhD in marketing from the University of Massachusetts Amherst. Before coming to LMU, he was associate professor at Northeastern University and spent the 2007 to 2008 academic year as a visiting professor at Maastricht University in The Netherlands. His research examines consumer usage and acceptance of new media as well as firms' use of mobile and social media marketing strategies. Professor Rohm has published in scholarly and managerial publications such as the *Journal of Marketing, Journal of Interactive Marketing, Journal of Advertising, Journal of Consumer Behavior*, and MIT's *Sloan Management Review* among others and recently coauthored the book *Herding Cats: A Strategic Approach to Social Media Marketing*, published by Business Expert Press. He is also cofounder and codirector of LMU's M-School initiative, a transformative and immersive undergraduate program focusing on the marketing, branding, and advertising industries, and has developed several courses for the M-School curriculum, including courses in social media and analytics and cross-platform content creation. Professor Rohm is the recipient of the 2015 LMU Fritz B. Burns Distinguished Teaching Award for teaching excellence.

Index

Page numbers followed by *f* indicate figures; those followed by *t* indicate tables.

OTHER TITLES IN THE INTERNATIONAL BUSINESS COLLECTION

Tamer Cavusgil, Georgia State; Michael Czinkota, Georgetown; and Gary Knight, Willamette University, *Editors*

- *As I See It...Views on International Business Crises, Innovations, and Freedom: The Impact on Our Daily Lives* by Michael R. Czinkota
- *A Strategic and Tactical Approach to Global Business Ethics, Second Edition* by Lawrence A. Beer
- *Innovation in China: The Tail of the Dragon* by William H.A. Johnson
- *Dancing With The Dragon: Doing Business With China* by Mona Chung and Bruno Mascitelli
- *Making Sense of Iranian Society, Culture, and Business* by Hamid Yeganeh
- *Tracing the Roots of Globalization and Business Principles, Second Edition* by Lawrence A. Beer
- *Creative Solutions to Global Business Negotiations, Second Edition* by Claude Cellich and Jain Subhash
- *Doing Business in Russia: A Concise Guide, Volume I* by Anatoly Zhuplev
- *Doing Business in Russia: A Concise Guide, Volume II* by Anatoly Zhuplev
- *Major Sociocultural Trends Shaping the Contemporary World* by K.H. Yeganeh
- *Globalization Alternatives: Strategies for the New International Economy* by Joseph Mark Munoz

Announcing the Business Expert Press Digital Library

Concise e-books business students need for classroom and research

This book can also be purchased in an e-book collection by your library as

- *a one-time purchase,*
- *that is owned forever,*
- *allows for simultaneous readers,*
- *has no restrictions on printing, and*
- *can be downloaded as PDFs from within the library community.*

Our digital library collections are a great solution to beat the rising cost of textbooks. E-books can be loaded into their course management systems or onto student's e-book readers.
The **Business Expert Press** digital libraries are very affordable, with no obligation to buy in future years. For more information, please visit **www.businessexpertpress.com/librarians**. To set up a trial in the United States, please email **sales@businessexpertpress.com**.